CW01335086

The Sky's the Limit

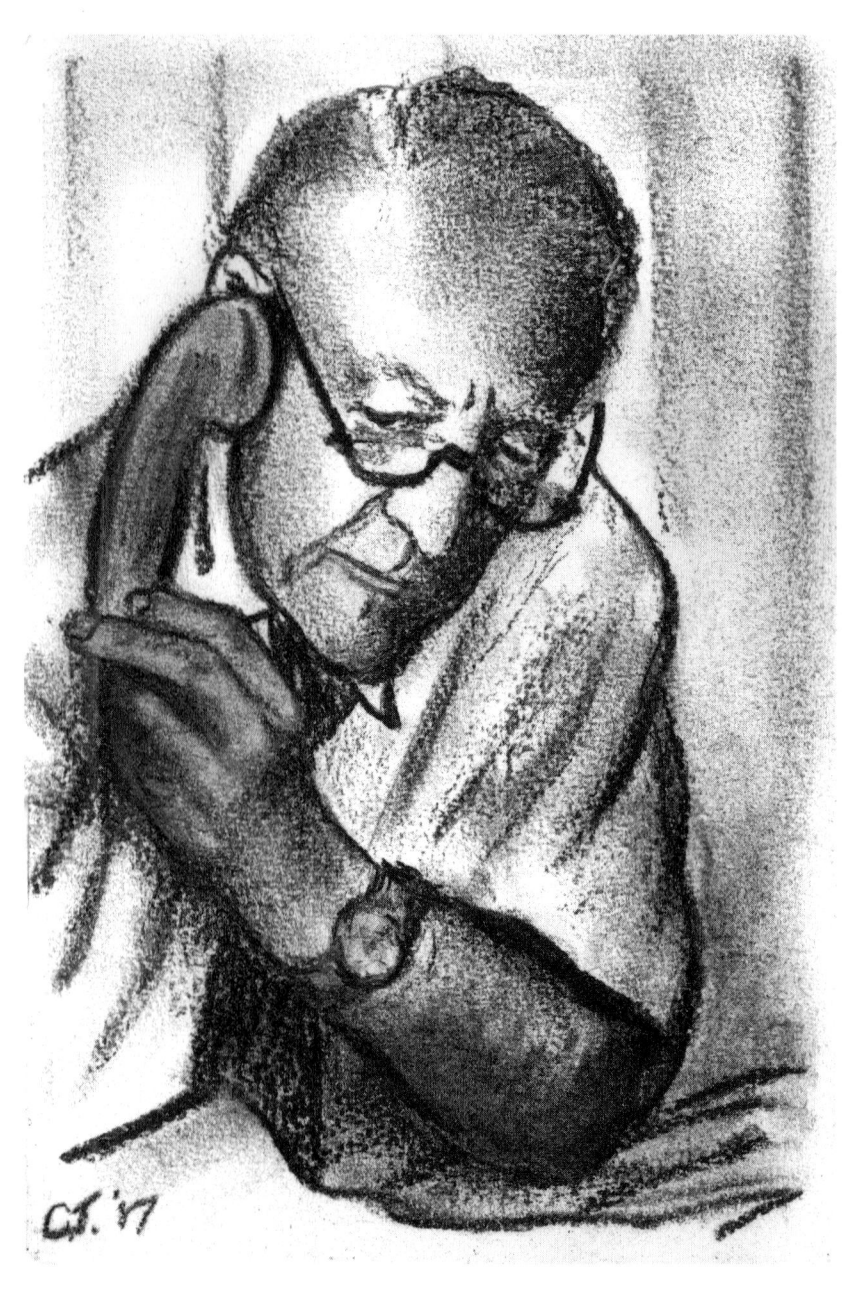

'JJ'. A portrait, in charcoal, by his son-in-law, Dr Clive Johnson, 1987.

The Sky's the Limit

The Story of
Bristol Philanthropist,
John James 1906–1996

by ROY AVERY

John James Bristol Foundation
2001

Published by the John James Bristol Foundation
7 Clyde Road, Redland, Bristol BS6 6RG

© John James Bristol Foundation, 2001-04-05
ISBN 0 9541316 0 6

Designed, typeset and printed by J W Arrowsmith Ltd, Bristol

Contents

	List of monochrome figures	vi
	List of colour plates	viii
	Acknowledgements	ix
	Introduction	xi
1	A Bedminster Boy 1906–21	1
2	Apprenticeship in Peace and War 1921–46	19
3	*Per Ardua Ad Astra*: The Ascent from Broadmead 1946–59	29
4	Flying High over Clouds 1960–68	53
5	The 'Sage of Sunningdale' 1968–79	65
6	The Making of a Philanthropist 1960–79	77
7	'Let's Keep on Giving' – the High Tide of Benevolence 1979–94	99
8	The End of a Life 1994–96: The End of the Century	119
	Appendix A	131
	Appendix B	139
	Appendix C	141
	Appendix D	147
	Bibliography	149

List of monochrome figures

frontispiece	'JJ'. A portrait, in charcoal, by his son-in-law, Dr Clive Johnson, 1987.	ii
Figure 1	Jack and Emily James – JJs parents.	3
Figure 2	A rare family photograph – JJ with his father, mother and sister, Ann.	4
Figure 3	John James Senior with his children, John and Ann.	6
Figure 4	The James' house in Philip Street, Bedminster – No 96 (far left). *(Reece Winstone)*	8
Figure 5	Bedminster 1909. *(Reece Winstone)*	9
Figure 6	The Merchant Venturers' School – 'The School to which I owed so much'. *(The Society of Merchant Venturers)*	13
Figure 7	School report, age 13 – an early step up the ladder.	14
Figure 8	Windmill Hill City Farm today incorporating the site of 96 Philip Street.	15
Figure 9	Corporal, Wireless Operator, Malta 1925–1931.	20
Figure 10	Top of the course, June 1925 RAF Marston.	21
Figure 11	RAF Base Communications Staff on Malta, Christmas 1926 JJ back row, second from right.	22
Figure 12	Servicing the Fleet Air Arm.	23
Figure 13	High notes in Malta.	24
Figure 14	RAF and Navy companions in Malta. Front row Corporal James (right) and John Besant. Charles and Bill Fiddick rear row left and right.	25
Figure 15	1980s reunion of 'comrades in arms'.	25
Figure 16	The end of his first career with the RAF.	26

Figure 17	JJ on leave with Mollie and his young family, David, Pat, Joan and Dawn, at the end of the war, August 1945.	28
Figure 18	Mollie opens a new Midlands store with massive help, 1953. *(Arthur Cooper)*	35
Figure 19	With Mollie at the Broadmead Companies' Dinner Dance in Piccadilly, 6 January, 1955.	38
Figure 20	The Annual Staff Dinner Dance, Broadmead 1950s. *(Bristol Evening Post)*	38
Figure 21	Daughter, Pat, May 1959.	41
Figure 22	Son, David, on holiday in Madeira.	41
Figure 23	JJ's two trusted lieutenants, Fred Farley and Ken Longstreet.	43
Figure 24	The Hub! *(James Russell & Sons, [photographers] Ltd)*	47
Figure 25	Chepstow, 1st May, 1964.	48
Figure 26	His favourite cartoon, *The News Chronicle*, December 17, 1959. *(Associated Newspapers)*	50
Figure 27	Happy and thoroughly at home in his pool at Tower Court.	66
Figure 28	In the study at Ascot. *(Financial Times)*	70
Figure 29	A silver salver, presented by George McWatters, to the man who saved Harlech Television. *(M. Wallis & Associates Photographic Services)*	71
Figure 30	With father looking forward to Festival night at the Bristol Hippodrome accompanied by Charles and Ann Fiddick. *(Bristol Evening Post)*	88
Figure 31	Waiting outside the Hippodrome. The First Festival 1963. *(Bristol Evening Post)*	90
Figure 32	'On the Prom' at Minehead 1963. *(Bristol Evening Post)*	95
Appendix C	Eight photographs forming an extract from John James' personal photograph album from Malta days with his own narrative.	141–145

List of colour plates

Between pages 56–57
Coach tour poster.
Keeping the accounts in pre-computer days 1950–1951.
Festival Music Hall poster.

Between pages 88–89
In the gardens at Tower Court with daughter, Joan, wife, Margaret, and son-in-law, Clive.
Daughter Pat's grandson, Charles, helps great grandfather do his crossword, September, 1990.
Tower Court, Ascot, Berkshire. *(Strutt & Parker)*
With daughter, Joan, and grandchildren, Elizabeth and David, at Tower Court.
His favourite chair for work at Ascot.

Between pages 120–121
Party time in Honolulu, January 1961, for sisters Dawn *(right)*, and Joan *(left)*.
Mollie fundraising for the scanner at Frenchay Hospital.
JJ outside the Royal Fort Lecture Theatre with the author after his Question and Answer session with 300 sixth formers, November 1980.
The house in the West Indies, *Rio Chico*.
John James CBE a proud day at Buckingham Palace with Margaret and Joan – 1981. *(K.R. Bray Photography)*
Doctors of Laws, the University of Bristol, in the Great Hall, July 1983. *(University of Bristol Arts Faculty Photographic Unit)*
With Joan at Breakers Row, Florida, 1983.
Backgammon with Margaret at Breakers Row, Florida.
Certificate of admittance as a member of The Incorporated Society of Merchant Venturers.
With Margaret at the Trust Headquarters, 1990.
A keen battle of wits with grandson, David. *(Maureen Dunn)*

Acknowledgements

This short book could not have been attempted without the generous help of very many people, all concerned to celebrate worthily the life of John James.

His devoted daughter, Joan, and his ever loyal sister, Ann, who sadly died shortly before seeing the completed story, and members of their families have been plied incessantly with my questions. Their sympathetic encouragement and detailed knowledge were crucial.

The vibrant and spirited community of his birthplace, Bedminster, guided me to the fascinating reminiscences of J.H.Smith and L.W.Vear, on which I have heavily relied, and to David Beasant, president of Windmill Hill City Farm, who kindly took me to Philip Street and to meet his senior citizen friends nearby.

Local and national newspaper reports and articles have been essential reading and are widely quoted with thanks. Special mention must be made of the *Bristol Evening Post*, which played a vital part in the organisation of his work for the elderly and which became a champion of his later achievements. The staffs of Bristol Record Office and of the Reference Library were helpful as always in providing valuable material.

I was most fortunate to have at my disposal the unrivalled experience and discernment of Michael Cansdale, Charles Clarke, David Dibben, John Parkhouse, Elizabeth Pennington, Gloria Powney and Lord Weinstock.

No one has ever had better facilities for the study of his subject and for hospitality than I enjoyed on my weekly visits to the Trust's offices. Mrs Julia Norton, The Trust Administrator, Mrs Joy Pike, who typed my illegible script, and Mrs Anna Pickford who put up with my incursions most patiently, were unflagging in their very practical support.

My sincere appreciation to everyone who has helped in any way with the preparation of this book, some of whom are named in appendix D, together with a list of the books I have referred to in my research.

The responsibility for mistakes and omissions is mine. Every effort has been made to trace copyright holders. If any inadvertent infringement has been made, the publishers wish to apologise sincerely and will be happy to make due acknowledgement.

My final debt of gratitude is to my wife, Marjorie, without whose understanding and reassurance the book could not have been written.

J. R. A.

Introduction

It is an honour to have been invited to write a short biography of John James, recording and celebrating his remarkable achievements. We are too near his own lifetime to make this in any sense a definitive work but it is not intended to be an exercise in hagiography.

His story is certainly a challenge. The wealthy as a class or group have rarely been loved throughout history. Aristotle and Plato denounced them for their greed. The prophets fulminated against them, dismissing their chances in an after life, and the followers of Karl Marx were ruthless enemies. The tabloid editors marshal their execution squads regularly to fire at the 'fat cats' in Britain today. The skills and sheer hard work which earned John James his fortune in, it must be emphasised, a pre-inflationary age, are ignored in a society where millionaires are created every week on television, or the stock exchange or the company boardrooms and the internet.

The individual philanthropists have scarcely fared kindly at the hands of the envious, the cynics, psychologists or social scientists. John James was far too realistic, far too honest to have any illusions on that score. He had studied the exhaustive examinations that had been carried out into possible motives for altruism. He had carefully made a note of them, 'guilt, the desire to be loved, the hope of eternal redemption, social competitiveness even social hostility to the point where acts that at one time were seen as virtuous and noble are now made to seem manifestations of a psychopathic disorder.' He learned that to give your money away, to set up a Trust to help others, requires self examination, the need to hold a mirror up to yourself and to your deepest convictions.

Nearly 2000 years earlier the Stoic thinker, Seneca, had written at great length on the moral and practical complexities of giving and receiving. John James passed his test on many counts. 'A benefaction is acknowledged in the same spirit in which it is bestowed and for that reason it ought not be bestowed carelessly. For a man thanks only himself for what he receives from an unwitting giver. Nor should it be given tardily ... and above all it should not be given insultingly'. 'Help one man with money, another with credit, and another with influence, another with advice....' 'What then is a benefaction? It is the act of a well wisher who bestows joy and derives joy from the benefit of it and is inclined to do what he does from the prompting of his own will'.

J. R. A.

1   A Bedminster Boy 1906–21

John James was born in Bristol on July 25, 1906. It was a significant time. He observed later that his birthday coincided with St. James's Day. Admittedly no plaster saint, he drew no moral from this except to urge everyone to visit the beautiful centre of pilgrimage at St James, Compostella. He could certainly respond instinctively to the Apostle's precepts to avoid snobbery, speak plainly and, especially to be 'doers rather than hearers only'. In the heyday of the British Empire 1906 also saw the launching of the all big gun ship, H.M.S. *Dreadnought*, and her cruiser counterpart, the *Invincible*. These were qualities of character that were essential for him in fighting the battles ahead.

His birthplace was 96, Philip Street, Bedminster, a small grey faced terraced house with three rooms upstairs, two down, plus a kitchen with a gas cooker, heating by a coal fire, lighting with oil lamp and gas mantles. The front door opened directly onto the narrow street over a well polished brass doorstep. It was a typical, very unpretentious home which housed the solid, working class community of Bedminster, proud of its traditional roots.

His father, Jack, born in 1884, had been a miner. He had already shown his sturdy independence in running away from school at the age of ten to get work in a local mine but had been brought back only to leave school two years later. There were 15 pits in Bedminster and Ashton and on the eve of World War I the miners' average wage of 5 shillings 6 pence 3 farthings a week was reckoned the lowest in the country. Jack left the pit in Deans Lane to move to South Wales, where he lodged with six other miners in the home of a colourful Bedminster barber, Charlie Stephens, who later attempted unsuccessfully to shoot Niagara Falls in a reinforced wooden barrel. Jack himself sustained a serious blow. He was trapped under the cage in the pit and was forced by the injury to give up, return to Bristol and on recovery eventually to become a docker at Avonmouth.

If Jack was the homespun philosopher father, who taught his two children, John and Ann, that 'if you can't get what you want, you must make the best of what you've got', his wife, Emily, whom he married in 1905, was the homemaker, the kind, hardworking mother whose facility with sums over the essential housekeeping money was handed down to John, a gifted mathematician. His sister, Ann, four and a half years younger, was the fourth member of a very thrifty, close knit family, teetotal and non smoking. Jack supplemented his pay with produce from his allotment in Sylvia Avenue and by occasional appearances as a singer in local concerts. Ann was paid the generous sum of sixpence for standing between another girl and her father whilst he stirred his audience's emotions with songs such as, 'And a little child shall lead them'. John went on forays with one of his friends, David Jacomini, son of the caretaker at Cox's Tannery, picking blackberries to sell at 3d a pound and so buy his long coveted pair of football boots. They also scoured the golf course at Knowle picking up lost balls to resell.

Life was a struggle for independence in the mean and overcrowded streets. The successors to the merchants who had left the noxious streets of old Bristol for the purer air of Bedminster had developed the mines, the tan yards, the lime and brick kilns, potteries, chemical and smelting works in once green areas. The beautiful and sumptuous Church of St Mary Redcliffe made a vivid contrast with its industrial surrounding parish. The majority of the boys left school to work in the pits or industry, the girls trooped daily to the large tobacco factories opened by W. D. and H. O. Wills, one at the end of Philip Street.

The struggle was not without its many compensations for the young family. Victoria Park close at hand was an oasis, a breathing space offering escape on hot summer days from the still air heavy with discharge from the local industries. John and Ann went to the park all day for picnics with friends. John enjoyed all the usual boyish activities there, jumping railings, swinging on trees, racing around the Park Ranger's house, vaulting park seats, pro-

A Bedminster Boy 1906–21

Figure 1 Jack and Emily James – JJs parents.

claiming the merits of 'Fatty' Wedlock, a hero of Bristol City football team. Bonfire night on the Plain was a huge entertainment also providing an opportunity to dispose of unwanted rubbish.

John would have shared many of the impressions and experiences of a vibrant community life with his contemporary, John H.

Figure 2 A rare family photograph – JJ with his father, mother and sister, Ann.

Smith, not least the river trip from Cumberland Basin to the steps opposite the Bristol Hippodrome. 'You passed the Mardyke Ferry and the training ship for boys into the heart of the old docks, in those days crowded with steam and sailing ships. Sailing ships berthed along the quays right up to the City centre; cargoes of hides, hogsheads of tobacco, locust beans, monkey nuts and a smell of tar and rope. What dreams of far off lands they conjured up in our boyish minds! A constant temptation to play truant and sport along the dockside quays'.

The sights, sounds and smells of his boyhood stayed with John all his life – swimming in the Malago, also a popular place for catching tiddlers, 'the smells of food from shops opening very early until late at night, mushy hot peas and potatoes, steaming faggots, freshly baked bread, the clanging local fire engine drawn by horses . . .'

'A walk through Bedminster before 1914 presented many sights which have long since disappeared. Horse drawn drays and railway carts, teams of shire horses returning to their stables, the horse drawn hearse proceeding to a funeral with bearers walking in front, wearing top hats and frock tailed coats. . . . Tram car trolley poles sparking overhead. . . . The ice cream cart with a fellow we called "Johnny Ice-cream" who played a concertina as he toured the streets. The old knife grinder with his pedal driven grindstone. The rag and bone man with his balloons and goldfish in exchange for rags, bones or bottles, the flypaper man with his sticky flypaper and his song, "Oh those tormenting flies, catch 'em alive!"'

The street traders and costermongers included Welsh women in their shawls balancing tubs of cockles on their heads. Families took their cakes or meat to the baker's shop and paid a penny to have them baked for Sunday dinner or tea. Sunday was a welcome day for dockers like Jack who worked 6 days a week. Every Easter John joined boys in the streets selling Hot Cross buns, carrying a basket and hand bell and shouting 'One a penny, two a penny, hot cross buns'. It was one of his many early lessons in thrift and self help from which he used to return triumphantly with a bag of buns for his family.

The day began very early for his father who, when he was not subjected to wretched patches of unemployment, rose at 5 a.m.

before his long walk 'down the Mouth', to the docks at Avonmouth via the Cut, some six or seven miles along the river bank. John's mother took him to school early at the age of three to Bedminster Bridge. There his class teacher initially was a very enthusiastic, energetic and caring woman, Mrs O'Brien, 'Paddy', whose husband played football for Bristol City. There were over 230 children in the 'baby' classes. John's writing which remained clear

Figure 3 John James Senior with his children, John and Ann.

and legible into old age, owed much to his early formal instruction. The 1911 syllabus for top Class I in writing included 'Capital and small letters. Words of two letters from dictation. A short sentence. Children's own names. Correct position (essential) during all writing lessons'. Class 1's Syllabus in Number, in which John was to excel all his life, began 'Count to 100. Notation and Numeration to 100. Add, subtract, multiply and divide by 20 with objects. Simple problems dealing with money. Dictation of numbers to 100'.

The log books for the Infants and Junior Mixed schools he attended reveal the poverty stricken backgrounds of some of the children. '20 boys supplied with boots by the Vicar', January 17, 1906. 'Distribution of soup to some 200 boys'. December 6, 1910, '38 breakfast tickets issued under the new provision of School Meals Act'. The Inspectors' Report for 15 June, 1911, summed up, 'The school is conducted with zeal and energy. The staff meet the special difficulties arising from the lack of any proper home training with cheerfulness, and show much sympathy with the children under their care. Probably the most valuable part of their work lies in the careful training in habits of cleanliness, neatness, obedience and self restraint given in the school'. The 1914 Inspection Report confirmed that the school was 'situated in one of the poorer parts of the city; the home surroundings are deplorable . . . one of the many ways in which the teachers strive to bring brightness into the lives of the children is by making the classrooms cheerful and pleasant, with flowers growing, plants and pictures, provided by their own enterprise. Improvement is to be noticed in many of the points in the last Report. The children's handicaps included 'meagre vocabulary, indistinct speech, lack of ideas and experiences'. One unusual experience was Empire Day, 1912, when a multitude of children formed a living Union Jack on the football ground at Ashton Gate, dressed in national colours and moving to give the effect of the flag waving.

The time came when he was seven years old to move on from Bedminster Bridge which had given him a good start. The choice lay between nearby Windmill Hill School and the more traditional, popular St Mary Redcliffe Endowed Boys' School. With the strong backing of his parents the quick-witted youngster entered the

Figure 4 The James' house in Philip Street, Bedminster – No 96 (far left) *(Reece Winstone)*

A Bedminster Boy 1906–21

Figure 5 Bedminster 1909. *(Reece Winstone)*

Church of England school with over 600 boys and 11 full time staff. The Headmaster was the redoubtable and locally renowned John Jabez Clibbens who had been appointed in 1909 and whose reign was in full swing. His enthusiasm was all pervading and, despite the acute wartime problems of staff shortages, he made his mark personally on the whole school. Very few were admitted from Bedminster and John found himself in the company of boys from much wider geographical and social backgrounds from within Bristol and beyond. The Head opened the school to many visitors who shared their experiences, often wartime adventures, or lectured on topics of concern. One on Temperance echoed the family's views. John was to come home one day and insist that Ann signed the pledge to shun alcohol, which she was obliged to do by her brother in red ink. Assiduous and keen he was certainly no 'swot'. He recalled, 'I had my share of the cane when I was at school. I don't think I was especially naughty, but I was in the sense that if I thought I knew more than the teacher I would take the mickey out of him'. The motto of St Mary's was 'Punctuality, Perseverance, Practice and Prayer', virtues promoted fervently by the boys' strongly Christian headmaster.

John was making very good progress when he and his family received a stunning blow – the death of his mother. The year 1918 witnessed a world wide, virulent epidemic of influenza which found easy victims among peoples worn down by the hardship of the Great War. Some 150,000 people died in England, one of whom was Emily James. The blow was all the more devastating in its timing. John had just been awarded a coveted Bristol Junior Scholarship, scoring 180 marks out of 200 in competition with over 500 candidates. He remembered, when in his sixties, his very confused mixture of pride and grief. 'I had a very great Headmaster. When I won the Scholarship in my year he took me in front of the whole school, laid hands on my shoulders and referred very kindly to my mother, who had just died. I remember thinking "this is a very human sort of fellow"'.

1918 was a watershed for the James family. Radical adjustments had to be made in their way of life. While neighbouring families were adapting to the loss of their men in the Great War, Jack at the age of 34 and his children had to come to terms with the loss of a loving and very capable wife and mother. Decisions had to be made which would crucially affect the children's personal relationships and development. The 12 year old boy would be in charge while his father was at the docks; he would continue to live at home and do all the necessary cooking. Ann at seven and a half went to live with her grandmother nearby, who looked after her well through the week until she returned to her father and brother at the weekend. Her bereavement was alleviated by her grandmother's care and by the companionship readily offered by the community at the flourishing parish church of St Luke's. A regular attender at Sunday School and parish social activities, she said, 'the church became my family'.

John's relationship with his father became ever more close and admiring. He learned from him how to accept misfortune stoically, how to live robustly and frugally and, above all, to stick to simple principles. There was nothing supine about the working class stock from which he had come. He was ready to cope with the big challenges posed nationally as well as personally by the future.

Lloyd George, the Prime Minister, flung the question dramatically on 4 November, 1918, to an exhausted and victorious people. 'What is our task? To make Britain a land fit for heroes to live in'. Jack's response in the light of his experience was hopeful, but realistic. Ernest Bevin was the hero of the hour for him and for his mates at Avonmouth. The Somerset labourer, youngest of seven children, had proved an outstandingly successful leader of the Dockers' Union. His speech to the Minister of Education, H.A.L. Fisher, that year captured the feelings of millions, 'The desire that their children shall have a better chance than their parents is inherent in the working class. The working class will only be able to emancipate itself when it has the power of knowledge'. Jack attended the packed meeting at the People's Palace in Baldwin Street on Sunday afternoon, 20th October, 1918, at which Bevin unfurled the Carters' Banner and the men and women of the Dockers' Union sang Lowell's hymn,

> 'Once to every man and nation,
> Comes the moment to decide'.

Jack was utterly convinced of the right to work but, if inspired and stirred then by Ernest Bevin, he was to decide later not to be committed to the new Labour Party's socialism or to collective bargaining and payment of union dues from his wage packet. He threw more energy into the quaintly named but very popular Royal Antediluvian Order of the Buffaloes. The Buffaloes were a Friendly Society for mutual support, the 'poor man's Free Masons'. There were many Lodges in Bedminster meeting in rooms over public houses. Jack became a minor officer. John and his sister went to social gatherings at the Royal Oak. They had vivid memories of the fun at the 'Buffs' Christmas parties at the end of which socks and shoes, scarves, gloves and clothes were distributed to members' families in need.

In September 1918 he mounted the next rung on his educational ladder, transferring to the booming Technical College established with great foresight by the Merchant Venturers' Society. It was a conglomeration of buildings in Unity Street, a great Hall, engineering workshops, laboratories, classrooms, splendidly rebuilt in 1906 after the major fire. The Principal, Dr, later Professor, Julius Wertheimer reigned for 35 years after his appointment in 1890, doubled the student population and achieved a brilliant, national reputation for success in science and practical subjects. He ruled by example as a pioneer, taking the first photograph by X-rays made in Bristol and providing the X-ray photographs in the first surgical operations. He became the first Dean of the Faculty of Engineering at Bristol's University College. One of John's Prefects, Paul Dirac, later a Nobel Prize-winner and outstanding theoretical physicist of the age, described the Merchant Venturers' as 'one of the best mathematical and science schools then existing in Britain'.

Any 12 year old, but especially one who had recently been orphaned, might have felt overwhelmed on entering this vast, buzzing institution but he was too sturdy, self-reliant and astute to let himself buckle. 'I was never made to feel self conscious about being a scholarship boy among the fee payers. I was aware of certain facts. I could not go to the tuck shop and, since I was cooking the food at home, I didn't take packed lunches. That didn't make any mark on me and I didn't feel any resentment'. Nor did his experience there give him any left wing views. Above all, the

Figure 6 The Merchant Venturers' School – 'The School to which I owed so much'. *(The Society of Merchant Venturers)*

teaching on the whole was excellent, he felt later. If he could not afford luxuries he could always show some initiative. He taught himself to play the piano accordion, mouth organ and flute to earn 'an extra bob' at local entertainments. These profitable ventures, he confessed, gave him a sense of satisfaction and superiority over the other boys and taught him two lessons in life – that if he wanted something enough he would make any sort of sacrifice to get it, and that he would always rely on saving and 'never go to the public for a penny'. The father's voice often resonated in the son's.

John flourished in the highly competitive, hardworking ethos of the Technical College and was top of the form at the end of his first year. His report suggests promise in a wide range of subjects from Mathematics, especially Algebra, to Physical Exercises, Geography to Singing. His prize for being top one year was 'The Gateway to Tennyson', which he kept all his life. On one occasion

Merchant Venturers' Secondary School.

Report on the Progress and Conduct of **J. James**, for the **Summer** Term, 1919.
Form **Upper Third B**. Number of Pupils in the Form **33**.
Average Age of the Form **13** years **6** months. Age of the Pupil **13** years **0** months.

SUBJECT	Position in Order of Merit	REMARKS
English	3	Good. EMC
Geography	1	Excellent. MC
History	4	Very Good. MGM
French	2	Very Good indeed. DMB.
German		
Arithmetic and Mensuration	3	Excellent MRH
Algebra	1	
Geometry	6	Very good. MRH
Trigonometry		
Freehand and Model Drawing	23	Fair
Chemistry (including Chemical Laboratory)		
Physics (including Physical Laboratory)	3	Very Good FWJM
Nature Study		
Shorthand		
Metal Workshop		
Wood Workshop	19	Fair
Handwork		
Physical Exercises	3	Good
Singing	9	Excellent

NOTE.—The Sixth Form is the highest in the School.
General Position in Form **1** Half Days Absent **8** Number of times late †**2**
Number of times reported to the Head Master for misconduct or neglect of work **0**
Conduct **Excellent**
Games:
Cadet Corps Work: *Very creditable*

J. WERTHEIMER, B.A., D.Sc., *Principal.*
G. R. CURTHOYS, *Head Master.*
Maud E. Hobbs B.A.
Form Teacher.

Next Term commences **Tues** day, **September** the **16th** 1919.

*Where two numbers appear in this column, the second number denotes the number in the set for that particular subject.
† When 'E' is added it denotes that for some special reason the pupil's lateness is, to a certain extent, excused. A number alone or following the 'E' indicates lateness not thus allowed.

Figure 7 School report, age 13 – an early step up the ladder.

his father came very proudly to the prizegiving with gleeful pleasure in the fact that John had beaten the son of his boss at the docks, Pugsley.

In the summer of 1919 The Merchant Venturers' Secondary School of over 400 boys was separated from the adult sections of the College and moved to Cotham, where the MVs' name was

Figure 8 Windmill Hill City Farm today incorporating the site of 96 Philip Street.

retained until 1931. The move caused some frustration to John's domestic timetable, especially the cooking. He now had to walk up Park Street and another hilly road to reach a bleak looking cluster of ex-army huts, serving as classrooms, laboratories and a large T-shaped shed used as an assembly hall and gymnasium. The younger boys were placed in the original servants' quarters of Tower House, a large residence in Cotham Road, where corporal punishment was administered on the first floor. Despite its uncongenial surroundings the school's reputation grew rapidly on the excellent foundations laid in Unity Street. Many of his classmates were to enter professions, law, commerce, science, education, like Professor Roy Niblett. One of them, the business man, Eric Packer, remembered a dramatic incident in which John had 'helped himself' to some sodium from its protective liquid bottle during a period in the chemistry laboratory. In the next lesson it burst into spontaneous combustion in his pocket. He rushed out of the classroom pursued by the master with the boys shouting 'Sir, James is on fire!' His main impression of John in the third form was of 'a boy in big clumsy boots and . . . I thought he must be very poor'.

In December 1920 a significant change took place in Cotham's grounds of which the boy must have been well aware. The famous Cotham Tower, formerly a stone observatory on a mound set in a circle of beech trees, was taken over by Bristol University. It was used for experiments in wireless directional research under the auspices of the Government's Radio Research Board. The arrival of this new technology on site was a symbolic event in the light of John's later career.

Paul Dirac, destined to achieve a world reputation, left school at the age of 16 to study engineering at Bristol University. John had already given notice in his turn that he would leave Cotham at the age of 15. Julius Wertheimer, who knew his boys' abilities and potential, wrote to his father urging him to let John go to university, Cambridge perhaps, or Bristol, where he was clearly capable of winning a place to study mathematics.

The question was a momentous one seriously to be considered but the answer was never in doubt. John's mind was set on leaving. He needed, and the family needed him, to earn more money and improve their circumstances. He decided not to stay at Cotham and to forego what to everyone at the time would seem a golden opportunity. A local example in the previous generation was J. B. White, a docker's son born in 1880 into a large family at Totterdown, educated initially at Windmill Hill School. He showed a flair in mathematics and had scraped his way up the ladder through Cambridge. He sought the security and satisfaction of a career in teaching which had just earned him the Headmastership of Queen Elizabeth's Hospital in 1918. It is arguable that a coveted degree would have placed John on the fast track to success and that he would have made his mark in the world much sooner than proved the case. But in what sphere of action? Understandably, in wealthy later life he never expressed the slightest regret at rejecting this academic passport to promotion.

This rejection in July 1921 was a defining moment. He was determined to take his chance in the university of life with its own rough and wide ranging examinations of character and ability and to graduate with distinction, *summa cum laude*. In an age of silent social revolution, the gradual expansion of careers open to talents, the slow recognition by society of an individual's worth, not birth, John James had pushed open the window of opportunity but only partially. As for so many of his working class generation his horizon was still limited.

The myriad experiences of the boy growing up into manhood helped to shape facets of his character and personality, his strong bonds with his father and sister, forged in adversity, his keen intelligence and curiosity, street wise resourcefulness and resilience and his essential stamina and energy. Unconsciously he was absorbing daily the folk memory of his close knit community, the teeming vitality and bustle of Bedminster. Like the East Ender's instinctive loyalty to 'London Town', the Bedminster boy's affection for Bristol was visceral, deep seated, though not uncritical. It was to echo the declaration made with feeling, perhaps exasperation, two centuries earlier by the great philanthropist, Edward Colston, '. . . but still I drew my first breath in Bristol'.

2 Apprenticeship in Peace and War 1921–46

1921 was a bad time for the teenager to enter the labour market. Full employment, which had existed during the war in which three quarters of a million men from the UK had been killed, had come to an end. In the summer, unemployment, which had more than doubled in the first few months, passed the two million mark in June. *The Economist* called it one of the worst years of depression since the industrial revolution began. John became a junior salesman and soon found the experience very unsatisfactory. His father who had himself run away from school, understood his son's eagerness to get away.

In 1923 John falsified his age and joined the new Royal Air Force which had been formed six years earlier from the merger of the Royal Flying Corps and Royal Naval Air Service; the first fully independent service among the great powers. He trained at the new RAF Wireless College and, as 356739 Aircraftsman James, J., was posted to Malta. The island was of crucial importance in Britain's naval and aerial strategy, which its people were to prove heroically in World War II. Britain then had no dockyard east of Malta which could handle capital ships. There he developed his skills over five years as a wireless operator, a most valuable experience for his later trading ventures.

John worked at RAF base Calafrana on seaplanes providing aerial support for the fleet. Many of the Fleet Fighter and Spotter Flight seaplanes disembarked there from their parent ships anchored in the Grand Harbour at Valetta. There was much activity as the number of aircraft increased and exploratory flights were made to Gibraltar and, more spectacularly, to Khartoum. His technical expertise increased and he received minor promotion after

Figure 9 Corporal, Wireless Operator, Malta 1925–1931.

passing out top with a mark of 90 per cent on a training course with 23 other aircraftmen at RAF Marston in June 1925.

These eight years in the RAF provided the background for his development from adolescent to young adult. He loved Malta. *Per ardua ad astra* was an appropriate motto for a youngster of spirit and attractively so when the stars in question shone over the Mediterranean Sea. Philip Street, Bedminster was worlds away. For years home leave was impossible but he always kept in touch and regularly sent home money from his pay, two shillings from his weekly three shillings. His father urged Ann to write constantly to him when he left after his first embarkation leave.

```
Casualty Form/Airmen/ Serial No. 71 dated 30.6.25.  Page. 4.
                          Trade and     — Nature and date of effect
    Number.     Rank.     Group.        Name. of casualty and reference to

"C" ABSENCE (Sick at Home)

330336.    A/Sgt(Pd)     F.A.E. 1.  Davison.T.L.    Sick at Home with
                                                    effect 27.6.25.

"P" ALLOWANCES AUTHORISED.

1257.      F/Sgt.        F.D.P. 1.  Sillitoe.A.E.   Ceased to draw Rations
                                                    in kind with effect
                                                    1.7.25.
                                                    ( C.C.No.2.(A.C.)Sqdn)

"R" RESULTS OF EXAMINATION BOARD ( Held at Manston 15-17.6.25)

    The undermentioned airmen gained percentage of marks as stated
    against their names;-       ( Authy;- Form 167 )

356730.    AC.1.    W.O. 2.      Janes.J.         92%
327134.    AC.1.    Turner.1.    Burton.G.A.      86%
343555.    AC.1.    D.P. 3.      Moss. A.E.       82%
351453.    AC.2.    C/Rigg.1.    Fudge. F.C.      64%
350548.    AC.2.    W.O. 2.      Haslam. C.       76%
356896.    AC.2.    W.O. 2.      Hunter. S.H.     61%
348969.    AC.2.    W.O. 2.      Knight.E.K.      61%
357389.    AC.2.    W.O. 2.      Mackie. A.G.     68%
355591.    AC.2.    D.P. 3.      Stockwell.G.A.   67%
353067.    AC.2.    F.D.P. 1.    Sword. A.R.      72%
348691.    AC.1.    R/Aero2.     Anderson.T.      68%
350389.    AC.1.    F.A.E.1.     Bailey. A.       71%
354029.    AC.1.    Arm. 2.      Barnard.J.G.     43%
354655.    AC.1.    F.A.E.1.     Barnes. C.G.R.   74%
357177.    AC.1.    Arm. 2.      Chidgey. A.H.    75%
350195.    AC.1.    D.P. 3.      Cox. R.J.        67%
333037.    AC.1.    R/Aero2.     Dryden. R.       65%
343730.    AC.1.    D.P. 3.      Foot. A.J.       65%
356464.    AC.1.    D.P. 3.      Forrow. R.E.     77%
335899.    AC.1.    F.A.E.1.     Gilbert. A.J.    62%
330970.    AC.2.    F.D.P.1.     Hills. F.        51%
346547.    AC.1.    D.P. 3.      Shrubb.W.G.      77%
362164.    AC.1.    F.Arm.1.     Stokes.E.F.J.    65%
342913.    AC.1.    Copp.1.      White. T.        43%

354981.    AC.2.    A.C.H.5.     Parsons.R.S.     Examined for remuster-
                                                  -ing to AC.2.Storekeeper
                                                  Group.3.
                                                  Marks obtained  48%
                                                                  /Contd.
```

Figure 10 Top of the course, June 1925 RAF Marston.

Malta was exhilarating. He could enjoy to the full all his favourite sports, tennis, water polo and above all swimming. He exulted with Robert Browning, 'Oh, our manhood's prime vigour! No spirit feels waste, not a muscle is stopped in its playing, nor sinew unbraced . . . the cool silver shock of the plunge in a pool's living water. How good is man's life the mere living! How fit to employ. All the heart and the soul and the senses for ever in joy'.

Figure 11 RAF Base Communications Staff on Malta, Christmas 1926 JJ back row, second from right.

The exhilaration and liberation did not mean indiscipline or promiscuity. With other RAF lads he formed a club pledged to the bachelors' self denying ordinance, 'No smoking, no drinking, no women', a trio of activities which were, he doubtless felt, a waste of money. His teetotal views then were very strict, based no doubt partly on the scenes he had witnessed outside the public houses in Bedminster on Friday nights after the miners and dockers had been paid. One of the young 'braves' in his group was Charles Fiddick, who was later to marry Ann, stay in the regular Air Force for the rest of his career and retire as Group Captain.

John decided not to renew his engagement of service but to try his luck and use the knowledge he had acquired as a radio mechanic. In his final year in the RAF he had met and married Mollie Stevens. It was the beginning of a marriage which lasted 35 years and grew into a family of four children. The young breadwinner began a series of short lived jobs, principally as a salesman in the radio department of Morse's store in Swindon. It was a frustrating time to seek any secure and satisfying employment. The country had come hastily off the Gold Standard and was in depres-

Apprenticeship in Peace and War 1921–46

Figure 12 Servicing the Fleet Air Arm.

sion with unemployment mounting to one in four. In 1933 the playwright Walter Greenwood wrote 'Love on the Dole', a prospect horrifying to John James and to his fellows. The following year Neville Chamberlain, Chancellor of the Exchequer, declared that the country had finished the story of 'Bleak House' and could now settle down to enjoy the first chapter of 'Great Expectations'. The country however became much less convinced of any happy ending as the government began to zigzag between policies of appeasing Germany and rearming for war.

John needed little urging to leave the drabness and the vicissitudes of shop life to rejoin the RAF in 1938. He was a young married man of 33 when the war began in the following year. In the light of his lengthy experience it was natural for him to develop extensively his skills in radio technology.

The RAF was also, congenially for him, the most egalitarian of the fighting services because it was the newest, its regulations permitting promotion from the ranks to an extent never secured in the Army and Navy. He was soon commissioned and finally became a Squadron Leader.

Figure 13 High notes in Malta.

Apprenticeship in Peace and War 1921–46

Figure 14 RAF and Navy companions in Malta. Front row Corporal James (right) and John Besant. Charles and Bill Fiddick rear row left and right.

Figure 15 1980s reunion of 'comrades in arms'.

Form 856.

ROYAL AIR FORCE.

STATEMENT ON DISCHARGE OF AN AIRMAN'S QUALIFICATIONS AND EMPLOYMENT.

Trade .... WIRELESS OPERATOR.

No. 356739. Rank Corpl. Name JAMES, John,
has been employed as, and is conversant with the duties of (*trade*) Wireless Operator
- .... in the Royal Air Force. He underwent training in this trade
at Electrical and Wireless School, Winchester. from 5th Mch. 1924, to 6th Apl. 1925,
passing out with 69 % marks on Final Examination. Since (*date*) 7th Apl. 1925.
he has been employed on the undermentioned duties, and has performed these duties with
the degree of ability as shown :—

(a) Wireless Operator.   Superior.

(b) -   -

(c) -   -

He also completed the following courses and obtained the results shown—

(a) -

(b) -

(c) -

Additional information as to the Airman's capabilities and employment :—

This Non-Commissioned Officer enlisted on 4th Dec. 1923 and underwent training to 6th Apl. 1925, subsequently being employed as a Wireless Operator until transferred to the Reserve. He is conscientious and hardworking and has carried out his duties with superior ability. He has qualified as a Wireless Operator Mechanic and has also passed Parts I and II of the Higher Educational Examination, obtaining a pass with credit in Part I. His character and general conduct have at all times been "Very Good".

Date 2 November, 1931.

                                             Flight Lieutenant,
                                             for Group Captain,
                                             Officer i/c Records,
                                             ROYAL AIR FORCE.

N.B.—This certificate is not granted to any airman who is discharged with a character which has been assessed as lower than " GOOD."

Figure 16 The end of his first career with the RAF.

Apprenticeship in Peace and War 1921–46

He was sent to the prestigious Royal Aircraft Establishment at Farnborough, the birth place of military aeronautics, known as 'The Laboratory of the Air'. He joined readily in the crucial development of radar which from its primitive beginnings in 1935 had progressed by 1940 into a sufficiently effective instrument of war to transform the country's air defence. This it did by offering just enough warning of an incoming attack and its general direction, though with far less reliability about its height and numbers, to enable a suitable response to be made.

The Germans bombed Farnborough once in the war, in 1940, in the Battle of Britain. So convinced were they of ultimate victory that they wished to take over intact this vital nerve centre of the RAF. It is a measure of John's worth, playing his part in the highly skilled innovative team at RAE, that he was able to move home with his family to the village of Fleet nearby for the remainder of the war. The work was top secret as RAE staff wrestled day and night with the problems of overcoming the Germans' blitz on major cities from heavy bombers to the later V weapons. Every kind of experiment was carried out there and at Malvern. Devices such as OBOE, a radar pulse audible to the pilot and H25, a radar scanner inside the aircraft giving a picture of the ground below were vital in defeating the blitz and launching the RAF counter offensive. John never talked about his work but it must have been deeply concerned with radar flying, the testing and production of airborne radar to help fighters initially, and then the bombers. He did reveal many years later that he had once equipped with radar the first Bristol Beaufighters flying out of Filton.

As victory became more evident with the launching of the invasion on D Day, 1944, John like millions of his fellow service men and women was straining at the leash, both dreaming and taking thought for his future. Life in the RAF was no longer adventurous and stimulating enough but it had given him great confidence and significant experience to face the world outside Farnborough. He had saved prudently from his officer's pay, while still sending money home regularly to his father, and was able to make modest investments in small shops, a grocers and then a drapers.

In 1946 on his long awaited demobilisation with a wife and four children to support he boldly bought the stock and goodwill of a

Figure 17 JJ on leave with Mollie and his young family, David, Pat, Joan and Dawn, at the end of the war, August 1945.

radio shop in Broadmead, the bomb-damaged heart of Bristol. Using his savings painstakingly gathered over the years and raising more money by taking a second mortgage on the family home he launched his Broadmead Wireless Company.

It was a momentous decision. 'It took me 40 years to get going', he recalled. The long apprenticeship was over. The radio mechanic had become a radio dealer. The Squadron Leader had taken the controls and in the exciting jet age ahead was to climb to altitudes undreamt of. John James was to become one of the most dynamic and successful business men in post-war Britain.

3 Per Ardua Ad Astra: *The Ascent from Broadmead 1946-59*

The brass bands and the victory parades had scarcely melted away before it became clear that recovery from the war would not be easy. The fruits of peace and commerce needed time to grow from the rubble of a blitzed city. The 1950s were to see a period of rapid economic growth, low inflation and virtually full employment but in the late 1940s fears of a short boom and a longer slump like that after World War I, vividly remembered by the teenage John James, were accompanied by a period of continued austerity. The new Labour Prime Minister, Clement Attlee, warned, 'we are going to face difficult years and to get through them will require no less unselfishness and no less work than was needed to bring us through the war'.

A prolonged bout of consumer rationing afflicted the long suffering British people for some years. Clothing rationing ended only in 1948, food in 1954 and coal in 1958. Items such as bread and potatoes, which were not controlled during the war, were put on ration. Some 30 per cent of consumer expenditure in 1948 was on items subject to rationing. The fuel crisis and the Arctic weather of the winter of 1947 forced the public to endure more austerity than in any wartime year. There were very acute shortages of coal and of foodstuffs from supply ships held up by blizzards. Unemployment soared temporarily to 1.75 million in February 1948, a bleak picture also for retailers.

John James was totally undeterred by restrictions and set about gathering as much capital as possible for his enterprise from whatever source – 'horse brasses, household furniture, groceries, anything' he said, added to the instant remortgage of his house, 'The Pines' in fashionable Stoke Bishop, purchased for £4000. His most memorable early sortie was the acquisition of a paint shop, Curwen Miller's in Newfoundland Street for £130. It not only bought paint but mixed it. He discovered from a discrepancy between the amount of methyl bought and the amount used with French polish that the Boer War veteran in charge was drinking the meths. This together with major shortcomings was vigorously remedied. A year later he was able to sell the shop for a breathtaking £10,000.

All his efforts were directed on his main target, the radio business which was ripe for expansion. Radio's popularity had grown steadily since the BBC's foundation in 1922 but by the outbreak of war in 1939 there were still some 13.5 million people, mainly from the poorer classes, estimated to have no access to their own radio. Mass-produced valve sets then cost £5–6 when the average weekly wage for a manual worker was little over £3 a week. Radios were becoming the new focus for family entertainment at home. A study of the impact on a working class area in Bristol found radio highly valued as a form of companionship, brightening time spent on housework, contributing to relaxation and leisure, and a sense of national identity, participating in the spirit and emotion of major national events. It had already gained some ascendancy over the press as a means of rapidly communicating news and information. Despite Sir John Reith's and the BBC's avowed intent to encourage a seriousness of purpose the most popular programmes were features with variety and musical comedy, music by theatre and cinema organists, dance bands and military bands. Comedian Tommy Handley and band leader Henry Hall were the radio stars. John James saw clearly that his business was to sell to the people NOT simply sets but essentially entertainment and enjoyment.

He rented his first radio shop in the suburbs at 38 Regent Street, Kingswood at 25 shillings a week early in 1946, following with the acquisition a month later for a few thousand pounds of the three shops of the Broadmead Wireless Company in Union Street. The owner, Mr Ben Turner, former naval commander, was a veteran of pre-war radio days whose experience included cat's whisker and crystal sets and 30 foot pole aerials. He shared his memories and advice happily with John James, who showed great judgement in picking a team of remarkable men for those pioneering days of the radio boom. Many were recently demobilised ex-RAF men with invaluable service experience in radio technology, ability as communicators and the willingness to work long hours in the cause. 'My men have permission of their wives to work late', he declared confidently. Foremost were men like Charles Fiddick, a senior RAF officer, his brother in law, young Fred Farley, Ken Longstreet, his van boy, Ivor Mines and Arther Webb, ex-RAF sergeant in accounts, his storeman who handled the clerical work and as storeman took in the radio sets. Their families were pressed into service. When a new shop was acquired in Bath, for example, JJ went with his colleagues, paint and paper to redecorate the interior over the weekend. While their menfolk were on the step ladders wielding brushes, his wife, Mollie, and the ladies brought frying pan and oil stove to cook the sausages and make the tea at the back of the shop, so that a brand new business could open on Monday morning, spick and span without losing a day's trading.

Painstaking reconnaissance enabled him to assess accurately the potential trade which each shop in a given location could achieve. He discovered the great variations between each area and its population. He did his homework very thoroughly, obtaining every available balance sheet of firms dealing in radios and reduced their often confusing columns of figures to simple arithmetic. Then he toured the country, driving over a thousand miles a week, studying the art of siting, window dressing, stocking up and selling methods. He discovered that there was a better chance of selling a radio set in a constituency which returned a Labour MP than in a Conservative seat and that there were important variations of taste and fashion in radio sets; what suited a worker in the Midlands would not go down well in London. He realised that many people who wanted a radio already had a broken set at home. He offered them the chance to rent a set if they would give him their old broken one which he then repaired. Very early on in his grand enterprise he introduced hire purchase, the golden key which unlocked the door to a million transactions for all classes of customer.

His four shops of 1946 had grown to 13 in the following year. The atmosphere of excitement and team spirit, born of much hard and well directed work, was reflected in the regular publication of an unpretentious cyclo-styled typed magazine of 20 small pages whose readers could well have been called the 'Broadmead Family'. Issue No.3 in December, 1947 began with the editorial from 'Uncle Tom' commiserating with the manager of the Kingswood shop, who had been ill in the Bristol Royal Infirmary. Ben Turner remembered the origins of his pre-war wireless experiments from crystal set to valves and his first shop at 252 Church Road, St. George, ending 'the future is with you all and I wish you every success'. A plain typed Christmas and New Year greetings 'to all from the office staff' contained the non-Nativity, minatory remark, 'we look forward to your close co-operation in all details so that the task of administration may be more streamlined.'

Two articles were by Charles Fiddick. He emphasised in dramatic terms the early morning rush at the Service Factory near St. Mary Redcliffe Church.

> 'Another day started! On go the lights, the side doors open and, as if by magic, a steady throb of feet denotes the arrival of the key men – the engineers – breathe it in reverence – the men responsible for more joy, and, very occasionally, more anguish in Bristol homes than the rest of Bristol's radio dealers can contrive in series or in parallel.
>
> They file in – strong, resolute men, each with a set purpose, an innate desire to reach the '4' mark to-day – or bust. The coats are peeled off, overalls donned, and all too soon the air is rent to high heaven with the piteous squawks and squeals of a dozen adjectival sets, intermingled with an occasional grunt of despair and whoops of joy as a white coated magician finds the answer to the electron theory – or otherwise. Some remember Ohm's Law and succeed, the others fall by the wayside but let's leave them to it. They've got a hard day in front of them!!! The Chief magician sets a hot pace.
>
> Meanwhile the Office Staff have not been idle. Like greyhounds trained to the minute they are raring to go. The bills printed overnight have been sorted out into

districts, and now comes the ripping of mail, the sorting of collection sheets, the reading of letters of appreciation from grateful customers with the heartwarming it brings, the OKs to estimates, the shrieks of despair from the agonised customers, the odd postal order, the rarer cheque – yes, the day has started.

Whrrrrrh – the phone bell rings – it's 'Jeff' with a painful reminder of 'overtime' and P.C. or else, and having surmounted that one, the shop staff usher in the first irate customer, who somewhat purple in the face – and obviously very liverish, demands immediate knowledge of the present state of repair of his set, collected by us yesterday. We jump at the chance of showing our prowess – 'T' produces the service number from one file, 'L' produces the answer from another, and a satisfied customer is ushered out in the space of thirty seconds – knowing that his set will be back with him within the space of another month. Good going so far!

Ha – the van boys have arrived!! Harry – you sweep the passages this morning. Tom, you do the office and Fred, sort out the shops – and soon the dust is flying high, wide and handsome, until Terry spies the first van – and races in to collect service sheets and sort out the first load. Soon the three van-men have arrived and the air is filled with tales of prowess, and groans of anguish as they recount the details of their encounters with the patient Bristol public the previous day. William is obviously very distraught – 'It's these ruddy engineers' he breathes – 'the way they gouge the sets is terrible – it's sabotage! I brought back fifteen radiograms from London last week without a mark on 'em, so you can tell it isn't the vansmen as does it!'

We put soothing syrup on to William, and sympathise with 'G' who's had two flat tyres and a broken door in the space of two hours the previous day. 'R' is more philosophical and grabs his sheets for the morning round before we realise he's arrived – and soon is followed by the others out into the loading bay. Direct confusion for the space of twenty minutes – cries of 'Fetch the Engineers' 'Give me the scratch polish', ' Where the Hell's number 3163' 'Fetch Ivor' – rent the air – the atmosphere is dynamic, tempers flare – and at 9.20 precisely, three furious van men appear in the office once again, just as irate customer no. 4 is ushered in!! A babble of voices all shouting together, gives the office staff just the feeling of power they need. It acts as a tonic – a satisfied grin appears on 'L's' face – he's in his element at last!! The telephone rings – 'Yungblood' breathes 'L' and the shouting dies. William recoils as if horror stricken, 'F' turns pale, his blood pressure dropping, 'G' leaves the office visibly shaken, only 'R' and irate customer No. 4 appear to have a grip on the situation. 'What about my set breathes 'I.C. no.4' 'What's this sheet doing on Stapleton?' growls 'R' 'Fetch Mr. 'F' and William now having had enough, disappears through the door – looking 20 years older! 'Yungblood' he whispers hoarsely – 'I could have sworn his set hadn't got a mark on it!!' 'My God – and to think I brought all those grams from London without a scratch . . .

Redcliffe Church Clock strikes the half hour, it's 9.30. Thirty minutes of organised bedlam has passed'.

A second article stressed the need for attention to detail, dates, addresses and district numbers on the service sheets, all instructions in RAF officer style, in seven crisp paragraphs, including no. 5, 'Don't think your branch receives a monopoly of all the moans and groans re servicing. We service many hundreds of sets weekly and the engineers are doing a damned fine job – and if you could see the effort put in by the chief engineer when passing out a set you'd wonder that it could ever go wrong again! The occasional one does break down shortly afterwards – due in the main to the breakdown of an old component – which appeared normal at test. It's this one that occasions all the heartburn – the hundreds of good ones spread our good name abroad. We want another five good engineers post haste, so if you know of a *good* one, let me know ac-dum. Remember he must be up to Broadmead standards'.

Figure 18 Mollie opens a new Midlands store with massive help, 1953. *(Arthur Cooper)*

His last and seventh point was heartfelt, 'Remember, we've got wives and children and occasionally like to get home before midnight!'

John James's hand was clearly guiding the selection of articles emphasising the dual targets of high technical skill and super salesmanship. An article about circuits, 'The Deeper Side of Wireless' by 'Oscillator', Ivor Mines, was accompanied by JJ's unsigned 'Random Thoughts' in which he preached the essential gospel to his employees, comrades on a great adventure, with simplicity and conviction.

> RANDOM THOUGHTS
> The first job of any business is to make a NET profit … to have something over when all the bills are paid. If it doesn't make a NET profit, then it folds up, and a lot of people have got to start again. Any business whether it's a socialist state or a capitalist's company has got to make both ends meet … and a bit over. Politically the trouble begins when deciding what should be done with 'the bit

over'. It will be one of the measures of our success if we do the right thing with 'the bit over'. But remember ... we've got to make it first.

One of the distinguishing features of a highly successful salesman is his triumph over the art of 'small talk'. His ability to talk intelligently and interestingly of just little every day affairs until – exactly the right opening occurs – and then – WHAM, another sale is 'in the bag'. Try and cultivate this art. Watch one or two of our smart salesmen at work. It could put 50 per cent on an ordinary branch manager's commission within three months.

The other day my wife said she could patch one of my shirts no longer and that I must take my coupons and buy another. Now there are probably more than a hundred shops selling shirts in Bristol, but I just couldn't make up my mind where to go – until I suddenly recalled a rather friendly sort of salesman in a Clare Street shop who some twelve months ago went out of his way to be kindly in helping me select a tie. He appeared to me like an oasis in a desert of salesman – and of course I went along and bought my shirt from him.

Now it's a pretty safe bet that, as you're reading this, there's somebody in Bristol who is saying, 'Where can I buy a radio set?' ... and he's probably thinking of a desert of salesmen too – unless he's ever been into one of our branches for a torch, a plug or some other little odds and ends'.

Over a third of the magazine was devoted to articles on leisure activities, 'For the Music Lover' (Ivor Mines) building up a record library from Tchaikowsky to Duke Ellington, all HMV products, 'Gardening' with hints from 'Jeff' on burning rubbish, grease banding the fruit trees and enlisting your wife's help, concluding, 'Happy Digging'.

Ensuring the goodwill and happiness of his staff and their families was a natural, instinctive trait in his ideal of management. His forbearing wife, Mollie, with their four children entered very readily into the fostering of a family spirit in the firm. She was more than understanding in her acceptance of the early sacrifices involved. There was little spare cash and no time for holidays in the early years. Saturday evenings found the family in the lounge with a blackboard on which the weekly sales from all the shops were telephoned in and recorded, the subject of a lively guessing game for the children. Later, wherever he found himself, at home or abroad, he continued to request that all returns were sent to him on Saturday nights. Arthur Webb recalled 'you never knew what JJ was going to do from day to day'. He once took Mollie to London for a day's outing, then seized the opportunity there to load his famous Austin Princess stately saloon car with radio sets, much to her discomfort on the return journey.

Mollie took part cheerfully and enthusiastically in developing the social life of the company, helping with teas at staff cricket matches, leading the dances and spreading the enjoyment at fashionable venues such as the Grand Hotel in Bristol or, later, the Café de Paris in the West End. She entertained colleagues and wives frequently at dinner parties at the Pines and was the life and soul with her own children at Staff Christmas parties, held at first in the Welsh Chapel rooms near the Horsefair. It was Mollie who helped with the washing up and made the jellies, the recipes for which plus her Household Hints she wrote in her 'Woman's Column' in the magazine. Her greetings to all wives and women members of staff wished them 'a Happy Christmas, even if it is to be an austerity one again'. This was the only reference to the appalling winter, the country's bleakest year. There was too much to do, no time to be disheartened.

This spirit pervaded the Social Club activities which included enjoyable evenings at Bedminster Police Station playing skittles, darts matches at The Duke of York, billiards and table tennis in the room at 21a Old Market which 'The Boss' had secured for them and equipped. Members were looking out for a piano, and kitchen facilities. The Territorial Army Unit opposite the BBC Headquarters in Whiteladies Road invited members to a FREE evening of darts, skittles and dancing on 9th January, 1948. The club's report concluded with warm appreciation of the enthusiasm and assistance of the young lady members. The amateurish magazine painted a picture of a lively community where everyone

Figure 19 With Mollie at the Broadmead Companies' Dinner Dance in Piccadilly, 6 January, 1955.

Figure 20 The Annual Staff Dinner Dance, Broadmead 1950s. *(Bristol Evening Post)*

was on friendly terms and 'the Boss' knew everyone personally. Homely quips were sprinkled about the pages ranging from 'Don't laugh too much at your wife's technical knowledge of radio; she might ask you to make a sponge cake!' to the prophetic choice of an appropriate gramophone record for individual senior staff – 'for our Managing Director – See The Conquering Hero Comes'.

If he were a hero, a title he would have rejected out of hand, John James had certainly earned the affection and respect of all his staff, over whose well being he took such great pains. In 1951 he showed his foresight and excellent judgement in recruiting an able young science graduate, Miss Elizabeth Pennington. She was to work with him loyally for over 40 years and play a key role in his financial success. By November, 1952 the 45-year-old John James had control of 115 shops and 750 employees. He had earned his first million. In a rare interview on November 24, 1952 he told *The Daily Express*, 'it is all a question of confidence – and confidence in the people you employ plus hard work. My belief was that if I was prepared to work when other people played I could do the job. This principle I have instilled into my "lads" and they have responded. Now with me they believe that people willing to work after the other fellow has gone to bed can build up a business every bit as sound as they used to in days gone by!' With this philosophy Mr James has promoted van boys and junior salesmen to directorships of his new shops ... He has taken the radio engineer from his back room bench and made him a manager in other parts of the country. 'For my part I see that my staff share in everything that is going – I believe in equity – that no matter what happens I, personally, cannot become any more wealthy than I am now'.

He had come a very long way from those pre-war Swindon days as a radio salesman struggling on £2 a week plus commission. He had never forgotten how his shop manager then had cut his wages back drastically when his extra industry earned him more commission than his employers. 'I never once had to ask him for a rise', said Arthur Webb, though everybody accepted that he had to give some priority to salesmen in equipping them with cars. The very strong personal, familiar, 'hands-on' leadership he exercised was vividly set out in his Memorandum no. 9 to everyone at the start of the New Year in 1952:

'Last night I caught my small son (rising 8) playing merry hell in his sisters' bedroom when I imagined him fast asleep. I escorted him back to his own bedroom and we discussed the matter behind a closed door (so that his sisters couldn't hear). As usual in these sort of affairs it was a complicated situation and he gave every indication that he felt a "general caution" (to include the girls) would meet the case ... Well, as I say, the whole thing was very involved and eventually we reached a decision. My son abstained from voting and received two whacks on his (by then, very cold) bottom. He darted into bed and remained comparatively silent. I then went along to the girls' room to clear up a few loose ends but, as you can imagine, I was too late ... they were fast asleep. All this time my wife and eldest daughter were at the cinema, and now as the house regained its peace and quietness, I went downstairs to my homework feeling I had dispensed justice.

But now I'm not so sure. Normally, I skip breakfast and make do with a glass of orange juice which is brought up to me by one of the girls. This morning it was rather late. I didn't appear over anxious to ask why but I gathered that they had been discussing last night's affairs. There seemed to be a wide gap between their interpretation of justice and mine. Later when the boy appeared chewing his sisters' sweets it became pretty clear along what lines they had dispensed equity. As most of you are married you can well imagine that the boy received additional compensation from his mother (who wouldn't have enjoyed the picture had she known).

Now you're probably wondering what in the heck all this is leading up to ... well, can I put it this way? ... The homework I was doing last night was a circular to all you fellows saying what a poor show you are making in trying to sell our "Sticky" stock. I felt like laying in to you pretty strong .... But after what happened at home when I thought I dispensed justice, I feel that if I do the same over these no. 4 sets Mr Farley and Mr Longstreet

Figure 21 Daughter, Pat, May 1959.

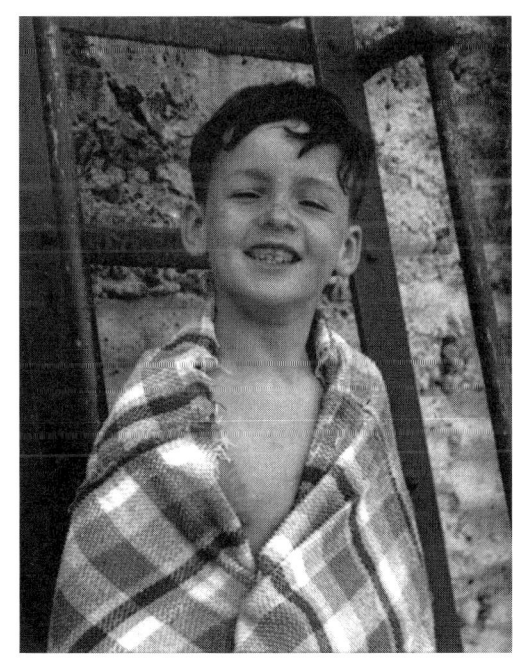

Figure 22 Son, David, on holiday in Madeira.

will come around with soft musical phrases and some of their sweet ration for all of you.

So I thought the best way was to write it all down just like this showing you how my hands are tied ... And shame you* into selling those "difficult to sell" sets.

Yours sincerely,
J.James.'

By the mid 50s the age of austerity was over, the age of conspicuous consumerism had begun. There was a dramatic increase in spending on consumer durables. The people seemed at last to be rewarded for their earlier sacrifices as the age of mass consumption began. New items like television sets were to transform the quality of life of the British home. The demand for television, given great impetus by the coronation of Queen Elizabeth II in 1953, accelerated rapidly, more than trebling between 1950 and 1955. In 1950 only one household in fifty owned a set; by 1973 more than nine in ten. Unemployment was very low at 2 per cent. John James incorporated the new TV sets rapidly into his stores, incidentally making the acquaintance, which was to grow into life long admiration, of the brilliant young Arnold Weinstock, son-in law of Sir Michael Sobell and future managing director of the huge General Electric Company.

He now had to delegate firmly and clearly his many responsibilities. In December, 1956 he told his 196 branches that he 'owed so much to those unstoppable men who joined me in the early days ... my mainstays in our struggle to reach the top. But above all two men stand out. They have performed well nigh impossible tasks ... they have stood ruggedly by me when the going was rough. They are F. Farley and K. O. Longstreet and now, when the foundations are deep down and solid, I propose rewarding them. As from today they become joint managing directors of our entire group ... I am as proud as they are. 1957 will be our "testing year", we plan an expansion of at least 100 shops in the next twelve months and, apart from a lot of board work, it should open

---

* The honourable exceptions who moved a lot of No 4 stock won't mind me 'blasting' those who didn't.

Figure 23 JJ's two trusted lieutenants, Fred Farley and Ken Longstreet.

wonderful opportunities for the lot of us. Our ten years' apprenticeship is over.'

He was right. 1957 proved to be the significant and testing year he foresaw. In May the company opened the largest radio and TV shop in Dudley, Worcestershire, Ken Longstreet's domain, with the conversion, costing £12,000, of the town's largest cinema in the middle of the busiest shopping area. As usual the reconstruction was carried out by Broadmead's own personnel. 'Electrical Trader', the National journal, was much impressed by the meticulous planning of this grand and novel project. 'Apart from the shop, which occupies what was formerly the cinema entrance, foyer and back stalls, the rest of the building is being used for other purposes. The balcony is being converted into a service department for new and second hand sets. The remainder of the stalls area is being used for new set storage for this and a number of other shops in the region, and for a dispatch and receiving bay. Other parts ... are being used to provide the service stores and component stores for the whole of the regional area, as well as the guarantee department for the area'.

'The shop layout incorporates many interesting features and is a further development of the 'walk-around' principle, which

Broadmead have already adopted in certain of their other shops. Down each side are displays of radio, TV, radiograms, portable radios and tape recorders, each a separate display and clearly sectioned. There is a further general display down the centre of the shop, thus providing two aisles. At intervals along the walls, are partly screened off booths with a chair and a table for customers to complete the formalities of a sale. The decorative treatment throughout is contemporary and the overall effect of the layout is to give a sectionalised exhibition appearance'.

'Opening out at the rear of this part of the shop is a big record department. This has a large number of portable record display units in wood, and two counter areas. One counter is for LPs only and the other, which is three sided, is split into a record, cashier and "inquiries" section, a "pop record" section and an audition section. Running right across the back of the record shop are eight audition rooms, completely built in plate glass and sound proofed. These contain only speakers, turntables being controlled from the counters'.

The crowd of 400 who had queued before the doors opened at 9 a.m., some through the night, received their reward in shrewd offers from Ken Longstreet, the choice of reconditioned television sets at 59 shillings and radiograms at 95 shillings with bargain prices for items all round. John James had planted another new 'state of the art' colony in his flourishing empire.

That Spring he had ventured to a far outpost of the Commonwealth, giving a well deserved holiday to Mollie on R.M.S. *Iberia* cruising to Australia. O. F. Mingay, an Australian journalist writing for the *Electrical Weekly* on April 26, was amazed by his story of efficient, technical organisation, salesmanship with minimum retail advertising, his policy of adding one engineer for every salesman appointed, his extensive travel by car through England and Scotland, his 'open market' practice. 'He pays cash in seven days and even before if he can get 5 per cent cash discount; and, get this one – he does not value his trade-ins in his balance sheet. They are valueless until sold.' He was impressed by his genuine modesty and lifestyle. Their 'four hour natter' was conducted all over iced water and coffee. 'He does not drink or smoke. He is quite a bloke'. Many aspects of life there were different from 'The

Old Country' but this 'fantastic successful retailing chain had obviously been built up on product knowledge, hard team work and unlimited courage. It surely shows what can be done if you set yourself a target and shoot for it. "Jimmy" James did just that'.

That June he made his largest single acquisition, the giant John Murdoch chain of 90 shops, worth £1million, its headquarters at Bloomsbury, selling radio, TV, musical instruments, baby carriages, shoes and furniture. The last three items peripheral to his concentration were trimmed away in an overhaul of the business but maintaining the chain's outstanding service to musical activities in the community and in education. In his earlier bids he had made the mistake of a direct approach, which had exposed his intentions to others who were in a position to outmanoeuvre him. He learnt the lesson that wherever possible he should acquire control by buying the shares in the open market.

The *Financial Times* strongly advised Murdoch's shareholders to follow the example of the board and accept his offer of 42s. 6d, a share for the rest of the Ordinary capital, Broadmead having already bought over 50 per cent of the Ordinary shares. 'When a good offer comes along like this, there's little you can do about it', said the Company's chairman, Sir Harold Gillett. On January 1 their shares had stood at 47s 6d; on June 12 the day before Broadmead's bid they were down to 39s. The deal had all been achieved, emphasised JJ, 'without a penny of outside help, not even a bank overdraft'.

The Murdoch takeover confirmed John James' company as the biggest single ownership retail radio-TV business in the world. Characteristically, he had flown to the USA for a few days' consultation with a rival claimant to the distinction in order to verify all the facts and figures with him. His American counterpart generously awarded the crown to him. It helped to make a golden summer after 10 years' unremitting effort. The new Prime Minister, Harold MacMillan, proclaimed the pervasive mood of optimism in the consumer boom, 'Most of our people have never had it so good'.

The striking advance had not been achieved without some conflict of interests. The takeover of Murdoch brought into the open the simmering tension with the franchises and the 'closed agency' practice. JJ from early days as a pioneer had come up against the closed agency franchise. In a large provincial city when he wished to buy a shop in a better location he found that he was debarred from selling certain brand sets. He accepted the challenge resolutely; all his instincts and 'open market' practice were against the system, as it then was. He retailed brands like Philips, Decca, RGD and Regentone, selling, he believed some 7 per cent of the entire TV radiogram-record player business in the UK. The 'Big 5', as the principal manufacturers were known, were worried. JJ, the latter-day David, armed not with sling and pebble but razor-keen mind and rapier, was undeterred by the industry's Goliaths. At the same time he sought to assure the owners of one man businesses that the 'struggle' between them and multiple businesses like his had been greatly exaggerated. Broadmead was a newcomer to the ranks and its pacesetting was essential to strengthen the industry all round and raise standards of service. With his own background he had every sympathy for the small trader, the major part of the 20,000 outlets or more in the country. There were, unfortunately, many independent traders who did not give such good service. 'The only difference between the multiple and the one-man business is time and a lot of well directed energy'. His provocative assessment led to considerable discussion in the trade journals, mostly on his side.

1957, the *annus mirabilis*, was followed by a time of reappraisal, reflection and crucial decision. He had acquired some 300 shops throughout the country, ranging from Aberdeen to Plymouth, West Wales to London's West End. Would the boom in TV sets and, to a little lesser extent in radio, continue? Progress was still being made. The *Financial Times* reported that, on average, individual shops sold 19 radio and 17 TV sets in October '59 compared with 12 and 14 respectively in October '58. JJ was a long way short of the target of 1,000 shops which he had set himself and his 'team of "amateurs" as we called ourselves' in the heady pioneering days, but he was far too realistic to tilt his lance at windmills. The chances he had seized so well seemed fewer, the risks riskier.

In December, 1959 he therefore sold out to Charles Hayward's Firth Cleveland industrial holdings for £5,800,000. He had met

Figure 24 The Hub! *(James Russell & Sons, [photographers] Ltd)*

earlier Charles Hayward, the chairman, a 'self made', good humoured and colourful character, some 13 years his senior. The fast growing group had control of over 20 different companies in five divisions, comprising engineering, electronics and instruments, steel, lead and retail stores, with over 11,000 employees and sales of over £30 million. Typically JJ had mastered all the legal expertise and knowledge required to transact the sale without the need to employ a solicitor. He was the first of the post-war generation of business men to sell out in this way. It is impossible to know accurately what £5,800,000 would be worth in current terms (at the Memorial Service in 1996 Charles Clarke estimated at least 25 times greater). He was to receive half in cash and half in Firth Cleveland equity shares plus a directorship. The Bristol flier had been welcomed aboard an aircraft carrier.

An assessment of his outstanding achievement and his group's was made in 1962 by Harry Miller in his analysis of 21 post-war British firms made for the Institute of Economic Affairs. Among its many assets Miller emphasised management skills. 'Of the 30

Before

After

Figure 25 Chepstow, 1st May, 1964.

people in the employment of the Broadmead Group at the end of its first year, 28 were in senior positions at the time of its sale to Firth Cleveland. What they had that people of similar calibre in a large organisation lacked was the notice and encouragement of their employers and a ladder of promotion with uncluttered rungs. Good management showed itself in getting full value out of the expensive service employed. John James, realising that first rate executives, however highly paid, might still feel tempted by going into business on their own account, retained the services of his regional managers by offering them the same privileges as he had allowed himself, first a winter holiday and next the use of a Rolls Royce or Bentley.'

'The outstanding feature of the Broadmead chain's rapid and substantial growth is that it was achieved entirely without benefit of capital from any normal sources. Apart from the plough back of profits it was financed by the purchase, improvement and profitable sale of several unrelated businesses and the acquisition of businesses for their tax loss advantages. This was an unorthodox expedient for so young a company to use, especially on such a scale.... While in less sure hands such a method of raising money could be risky, it is an interesting example of what can be accomplished by looking outside the obvious sources of business finance'.

The press had a field day as the news of the sale broke. The journalists were not interested in the subtleties of analysis of financial and management skills. Some had noticed, especially in the local press, that JJ repeatedly used the pronoun 'we', not 'I', when talking of the group. The headlines now focused on a great personal triumph for 'Bristol's modest millionaire', 'Ex-corporal sells shops for over £5 million'. 'The amazing Mr James', 'Quiet John James becomes a £6 million tycoon' and the inevitable 'Local Boy makes Good'. Hating the limelight he nonetheless enjoyed the opportunity of the enforced media attention to deliver some tongue in cheek comments. 'Problems in life can all be solved by mathematics'.

Tucked away in his own scrapbook among all the press gossip and photographs were four items which gratified him, a letter, two envelopes and a cartoon. The letter was sent by a Mr Kendall, a director of Classic Television Services Ltd., Croydon, 17 December

Figure 26 His favourite cartoon, *The News Chronicle*, December 17, 1959. *(Associated Newspapers)*

1959, 'Dear Mr James, Congratulations! You have taught everybody a lesson and shown just how little we all know about business generally, not just the television business.... What is more you did it all without the help of Pye, Bush, Echo, Murphy and all the other know-alls in the trade who, at various times, have predicted your downfall.... More power to your elbow and good luck, although you seem to have managed very well without having to rely on that'. Yours truly, J Kendall.

The two envelopes he retained were very simply addressed to 'John James (Radio Expert), Clifton, near Bristol, Somerset' and 'The Quiet Tycoon, Mr John James, Stoke Bishop, Bristol'. A cartoon in the *The News Chronicle* appealed to his sense of humour. It showed an irate housewife, brandishing a paper with the headline 'Man makes £6 million from his gratuity' and shrieking at her cowering husband in his armchair and the inevitable slippers ' ... and what did you do with YOUR gratuity? A night out with the boys, a couple of new shirts and it was gone!'

In the Middle Ages Bristol, city of churches and commerce, was second only to London in wealth and standing. In the middle years of the twentieth century after a second world war John James had hoisted the flag outside the old city wall, linked the historic name of Broadmead with that of Bristol and captured the country's imagination. These had, arguably, been the most exhilarating and happy years for him and his family. The dedicated and agile swimmer had caught Shakespeare's

'... tide in the affairs of men,
Which, taken at the flood, leads on to fortune'.
What next?

4   Flying High over Clouds 1960-68

The Bristol flier's voyage on board the Firth Cleveland aircraft carrier was to prove brief and discontented. The Headquarters of the big industrial holding group was at Stornoway House, a stately Regency building overlooking the quiet Green Park and St James's Palace, once the elegant home of peers and cabinet ministers. More recently it was the home (for 20 years) of Lord Beaverbrook, whom John James admired and he had reopened it after its closure through bomb damage. Charles Hayward, 68 years old, white haired man of three fabulously successful careers and John James, 55 the man of one fabulously successful career, met each other over the board room table. The story that at the first meeting JJ pulled out his watch and announced to his startled new colleagues, 'I can give you 40 minutes' may or may not be factually correct. It has certainly become legendary.

Charles Hayward was delighted with his major deal, proclaiming to his annual shareholders' meeting that, with the Broadmead Group, 'We now stretch from Aberdeen to Plymouth and possess the largest and most progressive retail group of this kind in the world and we intend to maintain our proud position'. There were bound to be difficulties in welding a progressive company into the structure of a huge group, especially when the new acquisition owed its success essentially to the extraordinary driving force of one man. Several times a millionaire, JJ could have retired with no further worries for his future or that of his wife and family. The thought never entered his head. His firm belief in the future of mass radio and TV retailing was as strong as ever. He was too strong an individualist ever to be the conventional 'good committee man'. Not for him the ponderous deliberations of lengthy agendas or meandering discussions following an excellent lunch. His darting, probing intellect abominated lethargy. Major differences of opinions arose inevitably over restructuring Broadmead within the company and over the very pace of retail development. He could never play second fiddle and so resigned with dignity in October, 1961, joined by his loyal colleague, Ken Longstreet. Charles Hayward was probably relieved at the departure of a dynamic challenger.

JJ retreated at first to his estate in the West Indies, Rio Chico, to contemplate the future and to see how David, his 18 year old son, who had recently left Millfield School, was faring with both property development and small GEC research projects. 'For the past 11–14 years I've been learning the business of business. Dig, dig, digging to start a career. Now I'm trying to put to use the knowledge I've gained'.

His first instinct, though not expressed in the style of Stornoway House, was characteristic. 'We are going to get our coats off and start all over again'.

His main assets at this stage in his life were assessed by one observer in 'Electric and Trading' as:

'1. Immense energy. The capacity to keep going 16 hours a day without let-up.
2. Concentration and an infinite capacity for attention to detail.
3. An intense curiosity about every aspect of business.
4. The ability, by sheer hard work, to make others work as hard with him.'

Other industrialists shared these characteristics but he also had the capacity to save. He was an illustration of the maxim that 'if you look after the pence, the pounds will look after themselves'. He echoed the great American industrialist, Andrew Carnegie. 'I put all my eggs in one basket. But by Heavens, I watched the basket!' JJ's frugality in areas of his business and personal life was to persist throughout his career.

Refreshed from the spell in the Caribbean with his daily long distance swims and landscape projects he returned as excitedly as he had been when starting off after the war. He applied himself to reconquering old fields, as well as trying new ventures, spending £1 million on 65 new TV and radio shops in Bristol, London, South Wales and the Midlands. By January, 1962 he had acquired 83 shops, 125 by March, selling sets mainly on the basis ' one year to pay and no interest charges'! 'The hire purchase idea is something of a gamble', he admitted. He was also drawing on the latest American technology with the newest electronic equipment to cope with the flood of paper work and HP agreements. He talked of having 500 shops by 1970.

At the same time his fertile imagination led him into more ambitious projects. He wished to buy up old estates with old houses standing in large grounds, which were only enjoyed by one family. He would build new homes, landscape the grounds (landscaping was his particular enthusiasm) and let more people enjoy the amenities. He attacked the developers who spoiled such estates by mass building and the cutting down of trees. (Asked once why he had no hedges around his garden at Stoke Bishop he replied that he enjoyed sharing views of the garden with passers-by). Hyndewood Development Company was created for estates in the Home Counties and West Country.

Also farsighted was his early, successful exploration of the media industry with its great potential. In 1961 he helped to launch the News of the West Limited to establish a commercial radio and/or television station under the chairmanship of W. A. Hawkins, Chairman and Managing Director of the *Bristol Evening Post*.

Shortly after the break with Firth Cleveland he met Mr Norman Williams, who helped to pioneer the furniture 'supermarket', and was converted to buying the Easterns Furniture Group, defeating rival bids in a large scale purchase with £2,300,000. Some sections of the quality press were patronising at first, deriding the very idea of a furniture supermarket and conjuring up visions of house wives pushing swaying pieces of furniture on trolleys. Easterns, an old pre-war family business, was soon booming with lorries shipping out the equivalent of 100 bedroom suites a day from one shop alone and taking back in part exchange old chaise longues, cabinets etc. JJ was exuberant after the success of his on-off-on again negotiations, a useful part, incidentally, of his own education in stocks and shares transactions. 'I am going to do a Marks and Spencer operation on the furniture industry', which involved employing 700 firms of decorators to convert Easterns' 24 stores into supermarkets.

A year later admiration took the place of snobbish scepticism. Williams Supermarkets were looking out for more stores, at least ten, in Central London. This would make them bigger than their nearest rivals like Maples and second only to great British Universal Stores in the retail furniture business. The brisk development was linked to a massive warehousing and distribution operation on the North Circular Road in London in a 280,000 square-foot former factory. Manufacturers' bulk deliveries of chairs, tables and bedroom suites were stacked in bays matching up with sample items which were all that the individual shops could accommodate. As orders came in, the loaders, instructed by punch-cards and walkie-talkie receivers, put the items on miniature railway tracks, which continually encircled the floor, and carried them to the waiting lorries outside ready for delivery. Williams planned to have the furniture put into crush- and scratch-proof containers so that they need not be touched again until they reached the customer's house, making significant savings on the usual retail price. It was far from plain sailing for the new regime despite the prevailing optimism. Williams became ill and resigned. JJ using a new young managing director, Leslie Ames, had to restore company morale and return it to profitability.

He was under no illusions that he alone could manage, lead and inspire in this exciting but risky period of experimentation. He needed help. His first shot was a dramatic advertisement in December, 1961. 'If I gave you a million pounds to build up a business, how would you spend it'? He shortlisted 30 from 1600 hopeful applicants and finally selected two for a probationary period. Peter Cresswell aged 29, came from the transport business; A.J.Henderson, 41, was an assistant manager with Southern Television. They both resigned within the year having found the targets and pace set by JJ too demanding. Most fortunately for him, his Bristol team, principally Elizabeth Pennington, Gordon Wood, Leslie Duck, Arthur Webb, Charles Fiddick were towers of strength. 'I would always prefer to have Bristolians, if possible,' said JJ.

DAWN JAMES CHARITABLE FOUNDATION

For those aged 70 and over residing within
THE CITY OF BRISTOL BOUNDARY
An INVITATION
FROM
Mr. John James and Family
TRUSTEES OF THE DAWN JAMES CHARITABLE FOUNDATION

THE OLD ARE NEVER ALONE WHEN SOMEONE REMEMBERS THEM

1979 FESTIVAL

17th YEAR

IF YOU WERE BORN IN 1909 OR EARLIER
You are invited to enjoy a
FREE COACH TOUR

Full particulars are on the application forms available from your local post office in the

CITY OF BRISTOL

or from FESTIVAL OFFICE in Minster House, Baldwin St., Bristol 1

• • • • • • •

Closing date for all applications is 19th January 1979

1950	JUNE 10	17	24	JULY 1	8	15	22	29	AUGUST 5	12	19	26	SEPTEMBER 2	9	16	23	30	OCTOBER 7	14	21	28	NOVEMBER 4	11	18	25
TAKINGS	4850	4428	4550	4668	4602	4270	4838	5002	5493	HOLIDAY 4355	4825	4841	5156	5283	5724	6307	6142	6104	5815	5897	5515	5805	5662	5334	5683
N°7	2604	2678	2514	2770	2693	2468	2483	2526	2528	2306	2497	2546	2650	2605	2473	2508	2663	2886	2525	2515	2484	2650	2655	2442	2365
BALANCES		14101																							
1	1169	992	991	957	835	1027	1410	1306	1572	1127	1371	1304	1140	1469	1445	1823	1764	1750	1191	1490	1500	1520	1465	1300	1309
2	428	237	400	326	558	122	245	402	468	357	288	302	549	447	749	804	722	525	1072	839	747	704	673	335	596
3	266	215	195	160	169	173	228	239	302	226	230	173	249	211	390	421	427	346	411	423	355	352	404	627	702
6	240	198	314	275	217	360	307	361	450	211	296	353	384	400	475	518	383	413	460	439	283	412	301	421	533
7	2604	2678	2514	2770	2693	2468	2483	2526	2528	2306	2497	2546	2650	2605	2473	2508	2663	2886	2525	2515	2484	2650	2655	2442	2365
8	134	103	118	150	104	117	160	163	189	109	143	158	182	145	162	203	165	152	151	167	135	145	156	193	164
					INCREASED M/F ↗												N°3 a/c	189	151	167	119	112	186	112	148
N° 2	4 / 120	3 / 101	5 / 93	5 / 116	1 / 102	2 / 66	5 H / 141	4 H / 99	5 / 94	2 / 69	7 / 140	4 / 74	1 / 62	5 / 112	1 / 76	4 / 153	6 / 92	5 / 108	1 / 95	5 / 116	5 / 105	2 / 92	2 / 71	4 → / 100	5 / 159
3	2 / 59	- / 36	2 / 48	2-1 / 134	1 / 69	2 / 73	· / 43	2 / 58	1 / 77	1 / 64	1 / 67	2 / 56	3 / 105	3 / 72	3 / 97	4 / 89	2 / 94	3 / 64	· / 61	2 / 57	1 / 73	· / 56	2 / 82	2·1 / 120	4 / 100
7	3 / 125	3 / 151	3 / 123	2 / 224	3 / 127	5 / 137	1 / 123	· / 122	2 / 191	5 / 179	3 / 130	2 / 144	1 / 111	3 / 119	3 / 280	5 / 193	5·1 / 241	2·1 / 237	4·2 / 302	4 / 165	3·1 / 168	2·1 / 172	4·1 / 157	8·3 / 381	3 / 162
9	2 / 89	2 / 61	3 / 67	5 / 126	4 / 107	5 / 109	5 / 77	3 / 90	2 / 100	3 / 86	9 / 119	2 / 68	6 / 101	1 / 63	3 / 93	2 / 122	2 / 102	3 / 106	6 / 168	4 / 131	2 / 103	5·1 / 185	2 / 92	2 / 105	2 / 102
14	3 / 166	1 / 137	4 / 169	1-1 / 126	··1 / 201	5 / 110	2·1 / 133	2 / 97	4 / 119	4 / 110	1 / 101	2 / 126	4·2 / 252	4·1 / 172	1 / 119	5·2 / 205	4·1 / 248	8 / 229	1 / 189	5·1 / 267	4·3 / 313	4·1 / 227	3 / 156	6 / 137	4 / 150
21	3-1 / 401	7-3 / 552	5-1 / 475	7·2 / 517	7-3 / 480	10 / 257	10·2 / 515	14·2 / 503	13·4 / 685	7 / 371	11·3 / 542	15·1 / 471	10·2 / 513	11 / 467	13·2 / 441	16·6 / 839	15·2 / 632	15·1 / 571	11·4 / 730	16·1 / 553	7·2 / 412	9·1 / 517	14·4 / 1021	15 / 695	8·3 / 1327
26	2 / 134	2·1 / 178	4 / 193	6 / 133	6-2 / 206	1 / 137	4 / 162	3·2 / 225	6 / 171	2·1 / 153	7 / 221	7 / 187	4·1 / 208	8 / 206	5 / 145	6 / 121	4·2 / 266	12 / 208	3 / 174	4·2 / 235	2·2 / 282	8·1 / 276	4·1 / 198	3 / 117	6 / 144
34	6 / 258	6-1 / 295	8·1 / 405	2·1 / 217	7 / 191	5·1 / 380	7 / 350	8 / 267	13·1 / 388	8 / 301	7·2 / 381	11 / 305	9 / 249	8 / 244	12·2 / 483	14 / 325	7 / 245	10·1 / 490	6 / 257	5·3 / 483	5 / 220	9 / 397	6 / 225	7·1 / 280	7·1 / 326
38	2-1 / 259	2 / 132	4 / 165	3 / 139	5 / 190	3 / 154	4 / 142	4 / 164	8 / 197	1·2 / 236	2 / 170	6·1 / 246	7·1 / 198	2·1 / 253	7·1 / 256	1·1 / 222	3 / 213	9·2 / 325	2·3 / 339	3·1 / 326	7·2 / 325	1·1 / 278	7·1 / 337	4·1 / 184	2·1 / 182
40	9 / 182	2 / 127	3 / 104	1 / 122	7 / 179	2 / 133	4 / 126	8 / 208	6 / 135	5 / 127	·7 / 145	6·1 / 216	2 / 103	6 / 166	6 / 179	5 / 184	4 / 142	8 / 252	5 / 113	8 / 167	5·1 / 236	11 / 326	2 / 122	3·1 / 172	6 – / 159
46	3 / 192	4 / 201	3 / 219	7 / 234	6 / 225	5 / 188	5 / 144	6 / 193	6·1 / 322	3 / 215	7 / 219	5 / 165	2·1 / 296	6 / 202	7 / 218	6-1 / 218	4 / 220	7 / 294	6 / 249	8 / 183	2 / 191	7 / 204	3 / 186	7·1 / 323	3 / 159
63	1 / 65	- / 85	3 / 93	2 / 79	2 / 115	2 / 110	5 / 136	3 / 114	4 / 126	5 / 184	3 / 124	8 / 125	3 / 76	4·1 / 295	7 / 145	5 / 148	3 / 114	5 / 126	3 / 105	2 / 96	4 / 142	4 / 133	·· / 71	2 / 90	2 / 90
70	1 / 121	- / 120	3 / 145	2 / 169	3 / 155	2 / 109	2 / 130	7 / 198	3 / 137	3·1 / 215	3 / 155	4 / 139	3 → / 152	4 / 172	3 / 114	6·1 / 219	1 / 120	5·1 / 226	5 / 143	4 / 196	2 / 108	5 / 140	4 / 188	9 / 143	5 / 123
76	2 / 72	- / 43	1 / 49	1 / 52	1 / 70	4 / 87	· / 55	2 / 87	· → / 52	5 / 101	6 / 112	1 / 67	2 / 91	2 / 101	3·1 / 142	2 / 92	1 / 160	2 / 64	2 / 64	· / 34	·1 / 52	1 / 84	2 / 87	4 / 50	3 / 60
109	4·1 / 224	5 / 133	- / 93	6 / 190	1 / 111	3·1 / 190	6·1 / 119	2 / 140	7·2 / 224	3·1 / 191	4 / 168	3 / 174	2·2 / 236	6 / 207	1·1 / 185	4 / 164	6 / 194	4·1 / 197	3·2 / 194	5 / 173	1 / 127	2 / 183	2·1 / 202	2 / 126	1 / 175
120	2 / 123	- / 102	- / 67	3 / 103	1 / 66	- → / 73	3 / 95	5 / 91	4 / 77	3 / 91	2 / 87	1 / 67	4 / 116	4 / 134	4 / 153	3 / 96	5 / 129	4 / 128	6 / 155	8 / 154	6 / 206	5 / 115	4 / 175	7 / 165	2 / 102
146	5-1 / 314	10 / 197	2·1 / 195	7 / 187	5 / 180	5 / 188	7 / 170	5 / 155	9 / 255	7 / 196	3·1 / 264	5 / 144	9 / 307	5 / 150	8 / 164	7 / 127	10 / 222	9 / 223	8 / 157	4 / 155	9 / 233	4 / 188	4 / 236	8 / 210	7 → / 193
256	3 / 106	5 / 94	4 / 107	3 / 137	4 / 111	4 / 175	1 / 118	2 / 105	8·1 / 232	3 / 82	5 / 124	4 / 100	4 / 115	6 / 168	5 / 124	5 / 123	5 / 115	5 / 147	4 / 110	4 / 262	4 / 94	7 / 152	4 / 107	7 / 106	6 / 156
348	3 / 129	6 / 168	3 / 153	4 / 158	6·1 / 241	3 / 128	10 / 176	1 / 128	7 / 203	3 / 155	6 / 117	5 / 188	3 / 141	6 / 185	5 / 141	4 / 156	7 / 340	3·1 / 169	3 / 153	6·1 / 244	3 / 187	3 / 130	3·1 / 214	3·1 / 156	2·1 / 144
OFFICE	274	279	272	297	298	273	279	268	257	237	265	281	260	271	278	293	270	290	272	274	297	308	283	304	286
																				B. W[illegible] GLOS.			1	812	638
																							2	103	188
																							4	225	280
																							S/H		
RADIO	60	58	60	69	70	68	81	81	108	73	94	93	80	94	97	104	94	119	78	98	75	89	72	103	78
T.V.	4	5	3	5	7	2	4	4	9	5	6	3	9	3	7	11	6	8	12	9	11	5	9	9	6
X's	1213	953	2648	2530	1215	944	1151	1579	1197	1090	1140	1268	1257	1135	1080	1004	2890	1194	1090	1174	1432	1181	1041	930	1147
X's / CASH	13568 / 56857		18746 / 66075		20905 / 74947		23636 / 84787		25922 / 94,635		28 330 / 104,301		30722 / 114,740		32806 / 126,771		36890 / 139,017		39154 / 150,729		41,767 / 162,050		43,738 / 173,046.		
4. 7. %	23.9		28.5		27.9		27.8		27.4		27.2		26.8		26.0		26.5		26.1		25.8		25.3		
LAST YEAR	22.6		25.1		27.0		26.6		26.6		26.8		26.3		26.2		26.9		26.3		26.4		25.9		
	10,004 / 44,247		13,037 / 52,041		16,144 / 59,726		18,009 / 67,518		20,161 / 75,568		22,333 / 83,266		24,044 / 91,549		26,303 / 100,682		29,860 / 111,062		32,099 / 121,962		34,885 / 132,700		37,259 / 144,132		
WEEK N°	10	11	12	13	14	15	16	17	18	19	20	21	22	23	24	25	26	27	28	29	30	31	32	33	34

Keeping the accounts in pre-computer days 1950–1951

THE BRISTOL HIPPODROME

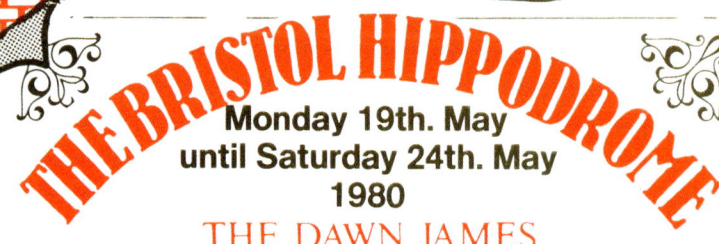

Monday 19th. May
until Saturday 24th. May
1980

THE DAWN JAMES CHARITABLE FOUNDATION

by arrangement with JAMIE PHILLIPS for TRENDS PRODUCTIONS, in association with THE BRISTOL HIPPODROME,

PRESENT

FESTIVAL MUSIC HALL

WITH SPECIAL GUEST

MOIRA ANDERSON

The International Singing Star from Scotland.

AND FEATURING

BURDEN and MORAN
Maids of Mystery - Masters of Illusion.

TED DURANTE and HILDA
The Premiere Old Tyme Strong-man act.

DOREEN HERMITAGE
From memory lane, nostalgia with a smile and a song.

FRANKIE HOLMES
"Who's a naughty boy?" Professor Frantic.

THE SIMMONS BROTHERS
The young masters of Comedy

ROBIN HUNTER
Your eloquent and charming host.

Dougie Squire's International Song and Dance Team

THE SECOND GENERATION

DIRECTED BY DOUGIE SQUIRES

THE OLD ARE NEVER ALONE WHEN SOMEONE REMEMBERS THEM

Key financial players for him in Bristol during this period were his contemporary, EJL, 'Ted', Parkhouse and his son John. Ted had come from a similar background of poverty and through hard work had achieved the status of a fully fledged stockbroker, attracting JJ's attention in the pioneering late 40s when he wished to buy shares in radio companies. As he flourished so he gave more business to Ted's small local firm which often had to work a 12 hour day. His son John, a former pupil of Bristol Grammar School, had vivid memories of JJ of whom they were both in some awe and whose negotiating abilities were legendary. Every day brought crisp telephone calls or visits to the office. John recalled taking a message from his father to the great man in his impressive office and telling him tentatively that he would like to become a stock broker. JJ roared with laughter and commented with feeling, 'Take it from me, you'll never really be your own boss!'

An accomplished chess player since his RAF Malta days, JJ possessed breathtaking abilities as a dealer, combined with remarkable cautiousness and astuteness. He studied the Stock Market painstakingly, was full of penetrating questions in negotiation and, understandably, pitched the price of his shares as high as possible on sale. A typical telephone instruction from him was '5,000 at 20 shillings, 2,000 at every one and a half penny fall in price.' This meant averaging his price lower and lower as the market went down and, as the market began to turn upwards, it did not have to soar before he saw the return of his money and made a profit. He always looked after his loyal and efficient colleagues and kept in contact with them. On his regular Sunday afternoon outings in the Rolls Royce taking his father to the coast, Clevedon and Weston-super-Mare he would call on Ted Parkhouse and his wife at home for a cup of tea. He invited them to his home in Jamaica and, *inter alia*, presented John Parkhouse with a specially designed tie with palm tree motif when he and his wife stayed there in 1972.

In this period of trial and experimentation with his first fortune he assumed several roles, some more successful than others. He saw himself encouraging younger men to do the executive work and he relished being a merger specialist, marrying businesses to one another and men to businesses. Making a correct assessment of the young men's potential and reliability was vital. He was proud of his part in GEC's takeover of Radio and Allied, the company that made Sobell and McMichael television sets. The chief negotiators of this huge merger in March 1961 were Michael Sobell, Arnold Weinstock, his son-in-law, and JJ himself. Arnold Weinstock became managing director of the huge complex and with a mixture of brilliance, prudence and hard work sent a huge wave coursing through the ailing company. His exceptional reorganisation skills enabled the quadrupling of GEC profits in less than five years. John James was a great admirer of the younger man and believed himself in some sense to be his sponsor and promoter. He never ceased to extol the virtues of share holding in GEC in good times and bad and to proclaim the qualities of a great British industrialist.

Family and friends, few, but carefully chosen were essential to his well being. He told a *Bristol Evening World* reporter in January 1962, 'If you have a car and fill the tank with petrol, you don't go on pouring petrol into it just because you can afford it. There is an optimum with money when it ceases to be useful. After that it is up to you how you use it and what you make of your life. The number of hours you work does not matter. It depends how effectively you use them. A problem can stick in your mind for months or you can have a sudden brain wave. In an hour and a half you can save yourself two years' work. Has money got very much to do with living happily ever after?'

His thoughts turned incessantly to his home in Bristol, though the necessities of business involved his long stay at the Dorchester Hotel where his frugal personal style (orange juice, cold meat and salad) drew comments on the marked contrast with the splendour of his Oliver Messel Suite. In July 1962 to follow Bridge House, he leased an office block in Baldwin Street, the old Western Daily Press building, which was rebuilt and converted into the prestigious Minster House at the heart of the commercial centre of Bristol. Roger Bennett, later to become a famous local radio and media personality, wrote a vivid description of the tall new headquarters and the new look in stone, steel and concrete.

Life was good. The press marvelled at his recovery from the Firth Cleveland breach. He was 'back at the top' with his new group of companies' excellent turnover in just over two years. He had become a grandfather. His second daughter, Pat, married Mr Steve Cranstone, a London businessman and provided John and Mollie with their first grandson and granddaughter. On 17 November, 1962 he again had all a father's natural pride and delight in the wedding of his eldest daughter, Joan, to Dr Clive Johnson, a hospital radiologist from Cardiff.

A few days later the press reported the major donation from John and Mrs Mollie James to the Lord Mayor's Christmas Appeal and to the outing of 85 old age pensioners after lunch to the Odeon from the outlying council estate at Lawrence Weston. There had been countless private individual acts of generosity before this, the first to attract the attention of the local press. They were heralds of an age of unfailing, practical goodwill towards the people of Bristol.

It was a measure of his accelerated progress and breezy confidence that he could afford to bid £11 million, though unsuccessfully, for the Firth Cleveland 470 radio and TV shops to whom he had sold his own group four years earlier. In 1964 he opened John James Investments, a £10½ million public trust in which his four children, Joan 30, Pat 27, Dawn 24 and David 20 were to have stock of £1¼ million each. This was accompanied by his proposal to offer £2½ million shares at 8s. each specifically to the people of Bristol. 'I felt that as I was a Bristol fellow, born here, and the people of Bristol have supported me right from the start, I'd like to see them having some of the benefits'. His dream was rudely shattered by the London Stock Exchange's veto.

The bitterest blow was personal and came like a thunderbolt. A telephone call to his home in Stoke Bishop in the early hours from the London police in April 1964, informed him that his daughter, Dawn, had been killed in a car crash in Knightsbridge. His family was devastated. Dawn was 24 years old, born in Bristol, educated at Winterbourne and Chipping Sodbury, and then at Saint Audries, a small Church of England boarding school in the West Country, where she had followed Joan. If Joan was the mathematician of the family, a school prize winner like her father, Dawn was the country lover, who kept pets and enjoyed pony riding. She travelled widely with Joan and they delighted in a 6 months expedition by sea to Australia. She trained as a beautician in

London and was both working and teaching there. Dawn, 'the outdoor girl', was also a keen reader who loved to write poetry.

The news was shattering. Mollie was grief stricken. John suppressed his emotions immediately. Ted Parkhouse telephoned him that morning. 'You know what I'm wanting to say?' 'Yes, thank you ... now what about those Murdochs (shares)?' was the unyielding reply. It was the biggest blow he had experienced since the death of his mother when he was 12 years old. If he padlocked his grief, he cherished Dawn's memory, kept her photograph always near him and framed a copy of one of her earlier school poems for him.

> 'The hours crawl by on leaden wings
> The earth spins onwards and going onwards sings
> of past and future days, the present time
> Is, of all ancient things, most great.
> What does it matter, whether tall or short;
> Lives are various. Through every sun and sort
> The things we do, and do to good effect
> Will, for our memories, great monuments erect.
> The passing fame will, as a bubble, burst,
> Leaving no memory upon transparent spheres;
> True greatness comes from inner man
> And greatness passes on, indelible
> Till worlds will end from time when time began'.

John James had already given abundant evidence of his wish to help his fellow citizens through his early donations to thousands of old age pensioners, co-founding the Old Folks' Festival with the *Evening Post*, and to the restoration of Bristol Cathedral. The numbing blow of Dawn's death was at once countered by the family's unanimous decision to set up the Dawn James Trust by which Dawn's share of the family's wealth was to be devoted entirely to charity centred on Bristol to her lasting memory. John would continue his career in business while maintaining a caring supervision of the Trust through his trusted staff at Minster House.

Life could never be the same after this shock, especially in the early years of mourning. He seemed to plunge more heavily than ever into the whirlpool activity of high finance. He always kept a cool head but seemed almost reclusive in social life, keeping himself very busy. Making money was always an exciting challenge. 'I still make many mistakes. About 40 per cent of my decisions are wrong. But, thank God, there are some damned good ones in the other 60 per cent'.

In July 1965 he made a significant change in direction, setting up John James (Industrial) Ltd as a holding company for small go-ahead companies in the South West, Midlands and South Wales. The Government's distaste for service industries and enthusiasm for manufacturing was clearly signalled. He aimed to acquire 'sound manufacturing companies with a sophisticated product and high quality management'. The rediscovered frontier of Bristol and the West was being opened up. The new motorways were rapidly integrating the South West with the major industrial areas of London, the Midlands and South Wales. The new Severn Bridge was hailed.

There was a choice of two policies for company collectors. One could either pay a fair price for small profitable companies and leave the existing management to achieve the desired expansion, or one could buy ailing companies and use outside management to bring them back to health. The second, sadly familiar in recent years, was rejected. JJ had no intention of buying headaches or getting involved in the line management of the companies he bought. He wanted to keep a competent management who wished to sell their ownership interest but would stay on long enough to train their successors. He stressed good export potential and set the investment limits for individual companies between £100,000 and £1 million. His target was a 22½ per cent p.a. return before tax on capital investment.

Who could help him in the grand design? He had been captivated by a leading figure in the Conservative party, a former MP for North Somerset with the panache and social cachet which JJ felt he lacked, and evidently with all the energy which he shared Sir Edwin 'Ted' Leather, 47 years old, Canadian born and bred, recently knighted, was bent on bringing the experience and dash of the new world to redress the balance of the old. He had awareness of the City and business and JJ appointed him as an ambitious and outspoken managing director of JJI and his deputy chairman. The Canadian set about building the new empire, while, characteristically, soon becoming embroiled in the local press over a dispute about parking meters and space for his Jaguar in a no-waiting zone near Minster House.

JJ also stressed his need urgently for three bright young men, preferably under 35 years old. The executive responsibility for finding and assessing companies for takeover was to be in their hands. His recruitment methods were dramatic and hazardous. The bright young men who emerged in the autumn of 1965, were Michael Birkett and Michael Cansdale. Michael Birkett, the 34 year old financial controller, ex-Sandhurst with seven years Army Service, had general management experience in engineering, hydraulics and construction industries after taking a degree at the London School of Economics. 'Business – it's all dealing with people'. Michael Cansdale the younger at 28, was an old Rugbeian, former Organ Scholar at St Edmund Hall, Oxford, a versatile musician who took a degree in Law and articles with a City solicitor. He specialised in company law, particularly takeovers and public issues. He had advertised in the Personal Columns of *The Times*. 'being keen to have a go myself' and was surprised to receive an immediate reply from JJ. Much impressed over coffee and a lunch at The Dorchester, JJ said, 'you should come to me', deriding all the normal impedimenta of written testimonials, references or telephone checks.

Later in 1966, when the Industrial Group was well under way, Ted Leather appointed the third member Peter Brien. He was a 32 year old marketing specialist who had sold overseas as sales head with Southern Television Company.

In the optimistic atmosphere of the 'swinging sixties' JJ organised his first two day conference for the Industrial Group and made one of his extremely rare public speeches in May, 1966 at the Brislington offices of the Iron and Marble Company. All his employees were there from managing director to foremen and shop stewards, workers' representatives. 'Where are we going? Standards must be set by people at the top, not those at the bottom. Don't imagine that the efficient few make only successes. They also make mistakes. I have a few scars myself (a reference to the heavy fall of shares in Williams Supermarkets). Mistakes are really only problems. You've got to face up to them. It's not the problems that matter but how you react to them and how you deal with them. To be successful one has to be not only objective but factual ... Don't use a lot of adjectives if there is no use for them. Make your meaning perfectly clear ... The sky is the limit. You name it, and if it is a rational proposition, we shall have a go. I will hold your hand until you make the baseline profit from which the real expansion can start'. Ted Leather then announced his intention to set up overseas trade missions, visiting countries with export potential and possibly exhibiting at overseas trade fairs.

All went well at first, though the young men were displeased at being labelled 'The Hunting Pack' by the tabloid press when over 90 per cent of their time was spent advising and working within the companies in the group. Useful expansion took place in the West and South Wales with plastics, high quality ferrous and non ferrous castings. Harold Wilson's Labour government incurred strong criticism, JJ attacking the 'creeping seeds of nationalisation and state control', reducing the incentives to work, the proposed wage freeze by George Brown, and the Selective Employment Tax which had forced JJ with great reluctance to close 30 of his 220 radio and TV branches.

Personality clashes within the 'dream team' became a nightmare for JJ who had had such high hopes. Ted Leather's ideas clashed with the more cautious and experienced magnate who found them excessively grandiose. He became increasingly unhappy about Sir Ted's trips abroad, his personal life style and, above all, his failure to deliver the expected profits. In September, 1967 Ted Leather resigned, overtired. He told the press, 'Mr James is one of the most brilliant men I have ever met. Working with him over the last three years has been most exhilarating but he is a man of very strong opinions and so am I'. Beneath the public surface was a deep clash of interests and a power struggle over the future of commercial television in the region. JJ was a leading member of Harlech which made a successful bid for Independent Television's contract for Wales and the West in July 1968, a great prize. 'Ted' was deputy chairman of the unsuccessful Television Wales and West board and thus in an impossible and unfortunate position. He left the rough hurly-burly of big business, became Governor and Commander in Chief of Bermuda (1973–77) and received honours for his public service.

It had been a bruising experience for both men. JJ bounced back rapidly, taking the blow in his stride, judging correctly that the company as a whole would not notice Sir Ted's departure because the investment side was prospering. JJ would become very wary indeed of politicians seeking to come into business. Harold Wilson was the target of his wrath. 'To drive our top men to pull something out of the bag we need a better carrot than taxation at 18s 3p in the pound. It is galling to see the government twisting and distorting my business to such an extent that we have to sack large numbers of men and women and at the same time see new Government departments created whose rising costs could only be borne by the industries they are strangling. It leads to a Rake's Progress and the survival of the fittest. Heaven help us if the fittest are politicians!' He admitted in October, 1967 that he had even, perversely, voted for the Labour candidate at the last election because 'it was imperative that socialists should learn that their theories would not work in practice. It was better to waste five years and get it out of their system … you can't nationalise anything and expect people to work as hard and efficiently'.

The 'stop-go' experiences of governments' financial controls were slowly leading him further towards greater concentration on the stock market and investment in manufacturing industries. This change of emphasis was symbolised by his purchase of Tower Court, at Ascot in 1968.

5 The 'Sage of Sunningdale' 1968-79

He now had to spend over half of his week in London and a home within Rolls Royce distance of town was infinitely preferable to a hotel. 'Not for him any extravagant night club excesses of the very rich' as Charles Clarke observed 'a house in the sun, yes, but no Mediterranean yacht, no string of expensive race horses, no vast accumulation of broad acres or the loss of a fortune on farms'. He took pride however in the possession of two fine Rolls Royces, which he much enjoyed. He also developed as a connoisseur of the best champagne, which, like his Rolls, he loved his family or close friends to share. Tower Court was a handsome five-bedroomed Spanish style house set in 45 acres on the edge of Windsor Great Park with outstanding rhododendron gardens, a lake and spectacular views to the south. There he could indulge his passion for swimming miles in his pool, and for landscaping. A *Sunday Times* reporter described him either by the pool in his trunks or in his 'workroom' opening directly on to the pool – a book-lined, light panelled room, a desk, and telephone, a pile of investment hand books, *The Times* and the *Financial Times* opened at the stock market pages and a rather grubby book filled with columns of figures and scrawled pencil notes. Neither in Bristol nor in London did he put up a protective barrier of personal assistants, accountants and high powered secretaries 'But I have to be quiet and peaceful so that I can think'. He was soon known as 'The Sage of Sunningdale', but his heart was in Bristol to which was devoted a significant part of the second fortune he was building.

The quietly spoken sage was certainly not afraid to flex his muscles when the situation demanded a real show of strength. His most famous gesture was provoked during the tussle over the

Figure 27 Happy and thoroughly at home in his pool at Tower Court.

establishment of Harlech Television, in which he invested heavily together with celebrity shareholders like film stars Richard Burton, Elizabeth Taylor, Stanley Baxter and opera star Geraint Evans. The HTV franchise was on offer and the Harlech Team were rubbished as men of straw by Lord Goodman on behalf of a London syndicate. The conflict between the two men and their supporters was resolved dramatically on the spot when JJ produced his cheque book to meet the demand. Harlech TV won the day. John's cheque was never cashed. Sir Alun Talfon Davies QC recalled, 'he was one of the most important members of the Harlech consortium on the West of England side. Nevertheless he was warmly appreciated on the Welsh side which included the Cardiff business magnate Sir Julian Hodge, creator of the Commercial Bank of Wales. His financial clout was a vital factor. Indeed at one stage the opposition were of the view that the financial resources of our consortium were inadequate to fulfil the terms laid down by the I.B.A. (Independent Broadcasting Authority). This was immediately resolved by John producing his cheque book. He was a person who spoke with authority and whose views were invariably accepted'. Harlech TV won the day and the future to provide entertainment, education and enjoyment to countless families in over a million homes in Wales and the West.

There were heavy black linings to the silver clouds. He was never under any illusion that money could buy happiness. He was disappointed in his son, David's progress. His stockbroker friend, Ted Parkhouse, died in April 1968, calling forth a rare expression of inner feeling for him in his letter of sympathy to Mrs Parkhouse. 'the heartbreaking news ... he had become an invaluable part of my existence, a man I could trust implicitly. I could not have had a more faithful colleague had I searched the wide world. He was by far the best man at his job that I know ... I shall miss him tremendously far more than I can say ... in some great part, thanks to his training, your son John will carry on where his father left off'.

After the death of Dawn, the greatest blow was the death of his father, peacefully after a short illness, at the age of 85 in 1969. He was absolutely devoted to him; he took him out for a drive every Sunday in his Rolls to Weston and Clevedon after giving him lunch at 'The Pines', and enjoying his favourite ice cream at the seaside. Of these keenly anticipated outings his father always said, 'He pays for the petrol and I pay for ice-cream'. They loved to discuss thoroughly their mutual gardening problems. Jack had never remarried since the death of his wife in 1918 and was very contented to be a proud father and grandfather. He never sought to intrude on his family. John built a small house for him in the garden of his sister Ann's Stoke Bishop home, 'The House in the Garden', where he lived his last 8 years and much enjoyed his reading and the contemplation of his flowers.

Two years earlier JJ, unusually on the stage, spoke to the crowded audience of Old Age Pensioners at a Bristol Hippodrome Concert. 'We were very poor. When I first joined the RAF about 1923, I felt it was time I helped my father. My pay was about three shillings a week. I sent two shillings home to him. When I got home he met me and in my hand he put a Post Office Savings Book. He had saved every penny and this gave me my first real start. He put some stuffing in me. No man can be prouder of his father'. A spotlight suddenly picked out and surprised his startled father sitting in a box over looking the stage. 'Don't thank me', said JJ to the old people, 'thank him!'. The funeral was arranged very quickly and quietly early in the morning at Canford in the presence of immediate family only.

1970 marked a major change in his financial strategy for the next decade. The financial columnists of the press assessed his interim position in February. The John James Group of Companies' performance, having doubled the dividend since coming on to the market five years earlier, offered a gratifying increase to shareholders, a total distribution of 6.39d (10.66 per cent) compared with 5.3d (8.94 per cent). The Industrial Group continued to improve with Williams Furniture holding its own, a good effort in view of the industrial recession. The big decision had to be made to sell the radio and television shops. The high costs of kitting out shops with new colour television receivers, the increasing competition and the government's change in 1966 from investment allowances to investment grants for which the business did not qualify were damaging. JJ was able prudently to confine the loss of £200,000 compared with the overall group trading profits of £550,000 in the previous year.

He therefore made the important decision to change to investment trust status. 'Full marks', said the *Financial Times*. 'The chances are that its suffering market image can only benefit from the move, aside from the material advantage to its shareholders of the substitution of a personal tax basis for the company's investment operation in place of the onerous corporate one. There was never anything ill-conceived in the group's philosophy that year-to-year in net worth (whether achieved in retail trading or security investment) was the measure of its success. The real place for goodwill or stock market expertise is in a management company's handling of fiduciary funds'.

The public reception of his decision was heartening. At a time when the City was perspiring, prices being drastically cut, there were no buyers but an army of sellers, JJ reflected sagely that 'as in all of life, emotions counted for more than slide rules' and proceeded confidently to employ his outstanding flair in investment despite the prevailing gloom and anxiety. His accurate stock market predictions proved beneficial to his shareholders. 'When we sold our stake (67 per cent) in Williams Supermarkets in October

1972 we took cash rather than shares'. The deal with Allied Carpets for Williams' 80 shops was for £4.6 million in cash compared with Allied Carpets' bid for £7.7 million. JJ nonetheless insisted on cash terms and saw his decision vindicated when Allied shares dropped from 270 to 180p and to 50p by 1974. Throughout stormy weather he continued to back GEC.

These were turbulent years for every facet of the community, from big business to the family. His own long and happy marriage to Mollie, the mother of his four children, ended in divorce. In 1972 he married Margaret Parkes, his faithful partner until her own death in 1991. In March 1973 he appointed to the Board Miss Elizabeth Pennington who had been his private secretary since the halcyon days at Broadmead. This was hailed as a richly deserved promotion for a very capable woman, who had unrivalled experience of working with JJ, always offering him the best and shrewdest practical advice, not least in assessing the personalities and potential of his colleagues or rivals, and moderating tactfully his occasional bouts of 'folie de grandeur'.

They were all plunged into the industrial showdown and the inflationary wave affecting Mr Heath's Tory government, culminating in the miners' strike and the General Election of 1974 fought partly on the burning question, 'Who Governs Britain?' JJ was in no doubt that the Trade Unions were grossly abusing their strength. 'If we placate the T.U.s we can get in the candles and tinned meat', he said vividly. 'There could be a General Strike'. Three years later in February 1977 he declared 'the T.U.s must learn that they must not inflict hardship on the community. That is quite wrong, as it was wrong for the old mill owners to throw a man on the streets without a penny after 40 years' work'. In 1976 his group, set up in 1965 with profits of £600,000 had achieved profits of over £9¼ million. The *Bristol Evening Post* reporter, Don Hatwell, asked him. 'Is this way of doing business moral?' Back came the quick, confident, sweeping reply. 'It is highly moral. We create wealth and we create jobs. In the past year our group created ten per cent more jobs. If every other company in the country had done the same, there would be no unemployment.'

The great vulnerability of the British economy was epitomised

Figure 28 In the study at Ascot. *(Financial Times)*

Figure 29 A silver salver, presented by George McWatters, to the man who saved Harlech Television.
(M. Wallis & Associates Photographic Services)

in the humiliating loan of 3 billion dollars from the International Monetary Fund, rampaging inflation at 25 per cent at the end of 1975 and the bitter Winter of Discontent in 1978. The much cited 'British malaise' was compounded by an overvalued pound, still bedevilled by the prospects that sterling could play a world role, excessive wage costs driven by trades unions alongside ineffective timid management, public spending beyond Britain's means to sustain it with any confidence'. W. B. Yeats' lines in the 'Second Coming',

> 'Things fall apart, the centre cannot hold
> Mere anarchy is loosed upon the world',

were quoted *ad nauseam* to illustrate the perceived disintegration of society.

John James' detailed forecasts of Stock Exchange prices and the FT index, his eagle eye for a profitable share, proved only too accurate and shaped his skilful course, not merely for survival but for progress even and expansion. Before Christmas 1974 he observed, 'It's easy to be a politician when, if you hit trouble, you just print more money. We are broke, temporarily broke, impossible to cope with a high inflation rate of over 20 per cent next year'. But there was optimism too for North Sea oil if its assets were judiciously used and if, above all, 'Britain takes her coat off'. For JJ there was always hope, his answer was never the despair of Yeats but the robust tenacity of Rudyard Kipling's 'If', which he had known since boyhood in Bedminster. He needed his measure of Kipling's ideal qualities, 'the Will which says "Hold on!"', the ability to "meet with Triumph and Disaster And treat those two impostors just the same".

Fame inevitably brought problems, personal and professional. Books have been written since Old Testament times on the precarious relationships of very successful fathers and their sons. His son David's abortive ambition at 31 to sail round the world singlehanded in his 30 foot yacht met with early disaster and ridicule in the tabloids. John James' fervent belief that his family must be firmly supported financially and initially encouraged but should then stand on their own feet, was tragically undermined when David, four years later, appeared at the Bankruptcy Court in Bristol, sadly owing to his failures.

It was inconceivable that JJ should escape jealousy and hostility. In an increasingly litigious age he had to fight and win two legal battles. The first was a claim by Charles Hayward, his former chairman at Firth Cleveland, who brought charges of misfeasance. The High Court ruled in October 1970 that the charges all be dropped and that Charles Hayward should pay costs. 'Quiet happiness and relief' were JJ's feelings as he celebrated with friends and colleagues over a glass of champagne.

Much more serious because of its very nature and attendant publicity was the claim for £1 million against him by Michael Oliver Birkett, who had left his job in the industrial division in 1971. He issued a writ alleging breach of contract and wrongful dismissal. There was a large sum of money at stake, enough to have a significant impact on the company and its reputation. An order for trial was issued in June, 1973 but it took a further two years for differences between Michael Birkett and his own solicitor to be settled. Mr Birkett, one of JJ's three 'bright young men', alleged that Mr James had promised to pay him a capital sum of £1 million if he could lift his industrial division's return on capital above that earned by the investment division. He claimed that he had achieved this by raising the profits from £30,000 to £300,000. The Queen's Counsel appointed by John James to defend him was Thomas Henry Bingham, a successful barrister later to become the Lord Chief Justice of England.

Judgement was given by Justice Sir John May in the Queen's Bench Division of the High Court of Justice on 19 March, 1979. The detailed evidence of Miss Elizabeth Pennington and Mr Michael Cansdale was crucial. Mr Cansdale was another of John James' famous trio of young men, the trained commercial lawyer who, after his 'apprenticeship' with JJ, had left to go into business on his own account in 1969. It was established that both he and Mr Birkett hoped that in the fullness of time, they would be beneficiaries from Mr James, 'in the guise of Father Christmas' added the judge. The burden of the discussions in question was about the challenge which faced these two young men, not about what their reward would be if they succeeded. The Judge warmly commended Michael Cansdale's evidence for its clarity and reliability, preferring it to both the Plaintiff's and Defendant's. In summing up he was fully satisfied that 'the Defendant had at no time ever agreed to pay the Plaintiff £1 million in any circumstances whatsoever'. *The Guardian* commented on Mr Birkett's, 'Walter Mitty-like dreams of making a million pounds before he was 40 and then of becoming Prime Minister or at least a member of the Cabinet'. The judge spoke of his potential but of his difficulty in distinguishing between reality and wishful thinking. 'Kipling again', JJ may well have reflected,

> 'If you can keep your head when all about you
> Are losing theirs and blaming it on you....'

He continued to develop his ambitions for Bristolians and the West Country while preaching his simple message in the national economic crisis. 'No speech by the Prime Minister, the Chancellor of the Exchequer, Jack Jones (the Trade Union leader) or myself is going to produce an extra pump or transformer or extra pair of boots for export. It is the producer who has to produce. The government must get off our backs'. He saw very early the future for foreign investment in Wales, putting £90,000 into the successful Japanese-Welsh factory Takiron at Bedwas, Newport. He appreciated Japanese managerial and technical expertise and was anxious to ensure that such investments could take place 'without so much as a whisper of redundancy'. He persuaded Takiron to choose South Wales, not Denmark, and was grateful for the active support of the young, local constituency member of Parliament in solving inter-Trades Union disputes, the future Leader of the Opposition, Neil Kinnock.

It was characteristic of his concern that on the morning after the lengthy and stressful High Court hearing he was back in Bristol again arranging further charitable giving to Bristol schools.

Two months later in May 1979 at the age of 72 he was set to 'call it a day' and end his hyperactive career of 'staggering profits'. The national and local press buzzed with speculation. Who was bidding for the quiet millionaire's inheritance? The Hanson Trust, trade conglomeration, was gaining national prominence and strongly rumoured to be a candidate. Bristolians were anxious about that Trust's doubtful reputation for asset stripping. The interests of the John James Group concentrating on West Country light engineering and manufacturing companies but ranging from building to boots and shoes, slide rules, iron foundries and plastic products, were a very rich prize indeed.

Victory was won by Wolseley Hughes, the Midland Group, the largest distributor of central heating equipment in the country. John James accepted their bid of £23,700,000, which was much higher than the experts in the City had been forecasting. He was naturally delighted. 'It's a wonderful deal for the shareholders and a great deal for the staff. Wolseley Hughes have agreed to carry on all the factories. There will be no redundancies'. Wolseley Hughes wisely recruited to their board of directors David Dibben, one of John James' most successful protégés, the managing director of his Industrial Group. He took responsibility for the former John James Companies with him and went on to create a multi-billion dollar enterprise with 470 branches and 11,000 employees for Wolseley Hughes in the USA. John James and Miss Pennington were to resign as directors. The Dawn James Foundation bought the group's preference shares and other investment portfolios for a net £7,340,000.

'John James bows out with a flourish', said the headline in the *London Evening News* on 30 June, 1979. His had been a breathtaking achievement. Throughout the 'swinging sixties' and 'the discontented seventies' he had travelled constantly between London and Bristol, the Sage of Sunningdale and the Benefactor of Baldwin Street, weaving between high financial operations and charitable giving. He had experienced vicissitudes, personal and business, yet maintaining his optimism and relishing the many challenges that confronted him, like a swimmer riding the waves to shore instead of vainly struggling with them. He had triumphed like the survivor in Shakespeare's 'Tempest'.

> 'I saw him beat the surges under him
> And ride upon their backs. He trod the water
> Whose enmity he flung aside, and breasted
> The surge most swol'n that met him. His bold head
> Bore the contentious waves he kept and oared
> Himself with his good arms in lusty stroke
> To the shore'.

John James' swimming, like his flying, days were certainly not over.

6   *The Making of a Philanthropist 1960–79*

'I was a Bristol fellow, born here … the people of Bristol have supported me right from the start. I'd like to see them having some of the benefits'. John James' benevolence first attracted the attention of the local press shortly before Christmas, 1962. There had been countless personal acts of generosity before then, heralds of an age of unfailing, practical goodwill towards the people of his native city. Further afield he was supporting Jamaican school and health projects from his retreat at Rio Chico.

In his 50s, embarking on his financial high flying in London, he reflected on the experiences of a man he admired, William Morris, later Lord Nuffield, who had written at a similar age. 'The man who would give money away is compelled to do a great deal of hard thinking. Is his gift going to do harm or good? Money has tremendous power and can do either. The responsibility of the would-be giver is great. If he is a decent man, he cannot escape it. I find a similar difficulty in lending money. Is it going to help the borrower or land him in a worse position next week? … To every man worth his salt the desire for personal gain is not the chief reason for working. It is that desire to achieve, to be a success, to make his job something worthy of his mettle and self respect. Money plays an important part in this – it is stupid to deny it – but it is the part of air to living things.'

'Why should you keep on worrying?,' the bachelor industrialist asked other men of means. 'The best thing you can do with money is give it away. Rich men don't give nearly enough money away. Why keep it? What can you do with it? You can only wear one suit at a time, you can only eat one meal at a time. You can lose even the pleasure of wishing for things'. JJ heartily endorsed these sentiments, confiding cheerfully in a BBC interview in 1968 that he did not have thirty pairs of shoes, only two, and that he had had to borrow a suit to come to the studio. 'Made in Bristol, not Savile Row', he added typically.

One trait of his giving was his earnest wish 'to spur people on rather than bale them out'. When the nurses at the Bristol Royal Infirmary started a campaign to raise £4,000 for a new kidney machine, he gave them £1,000 immediately. 'To have bought it outright for them', he reasoned, 'would have robbed them of their own initiative and pride. They raised the rest'. When a local Nursing Home needing two new operating theatres had done everything possible to raise the money, he came with the Dawn James Foundation to provide the sum remaining, £20,000.

'Accumulate, meditate, donate', could well have been his watch words. The first focus of his vision for the community, instinctively shared by Mollie and the family was the welfare of the old. His deep affection for his father, 'there is not a son in Bristol, nor indeed in England, who is as proud of his father as I am', radiated in his giving throughout Bristol. 'The real power of money is to be able to help people – to take their worries away.' In the optimistic, tumultuous decade of 'the swinging sixties', when the attention of the public was captured by the Beatle worship and activities of the young, John James and Mollie were flying a large flag for the elderly 'who', he said, 'cannot always battle on their own whilst there are many organisations helping the children'. Keen as he was to stimulate others to fend for themselves, he felt strongly that people in their 70s could not create their own money and must be helped to a decent life. He was already concerned that the problems of old age would increase relentlessly in the next century with greater longevity and that old people 'must never be thrown on the scrap heap'.

Bricks and mortar never deeply engaged his real enthusiasm and altruism. It was people themselves, especially old people at first, with their unique and amazing varieties of character and experience, their hopes and hardships, who enlisted his keen interest and sympathy, and whom he often found inspiring. These were the men and women who had grown up in the age of Queen Victoria and Mr Gladstone, who had left their elementary board schools at 11 or 12. They had made their way in a society where the average life expectancy was 50 and where the concept of a 'Welfare State' was Utopian fantasy. They were in essence his father, Jack, his aunt and uncle, his neighbours in Philip Street, Bedminster and far beyond.

Why not give them all 'a good treat', a day out to enjoy and a good show to entertain them in music hall style? His father's delight in their Sunday trips to the coast convinced him that such a venture would be immensely worthwhile. It was an almost wild, breathtaking idea, most daunting to the faint hearted in the complexity of the logistics. It required a John James to imagine such an operation and his good fortune in turning for help to the *Bristol Evening Post* and their managing editor, Colonel F. J. Harrison. His administrative ability, reinforced by his army and commercial experience, was to prove equal to the great challenge to pioneer an unprecedented scheme. His factual Report to John James and to the Bristol Round Table conveyed fully the problems he had to face and the first solutions which he engineered.

> '1963
>
> The Bristol Old Folks' Festival Week was held this year from May 19 to May 26 and was the outcome of an original idea of Mr and Mrs John James. It was made possible by their personal gift of some £12,000 to meet the cost.
>
> At the request of Mr James, the *Bristol Evening Post* undertook to organise the Festival Week, and I was given the task of putting it into effect. I am sure you will appreciate, when you have heard about the Festival, why we have found it necessary to have a full time paid organiser this year. It meant that I had to be seconded more or less entirely, from my normal duties for some months in connection with the organisation, and the managing director feels that we cannot have a member of the staff tied up to this extent every year. I shall however, be available in any advisory capacity required to the appointed organiser and anyone else concerned with

the running of the Festival, so that the lessons of last year will not be lost.

It was very right, I am sure, that the *Evening Post* should undertake the organisation of the first Festival because it was in many ways experimental and a newspaper's shoulders are certainly broad enough to carry any criticisms. In fact, the whole thing was very successful, which resulted in Mr James's wish that it should take place every year.

Some of the problems of organisation which had to be overcome can be appreciated from the following facts:

In the Bristol area, including Kingswood, Warmley, Mangotsfield and Keynsham, there were 56,000 persons over 65 years of age and 35,500 over 70 at the last census – and the questions we had to ask ourselves were:

1. What area should we cover?
2. What age groups could we include?
3. What types of free entertainment should we provide and how many types?
4. At what time should we hold the Festival week?

All these factors had to be reconciled with the amount of money available.

As regards:

1. The area group – we felt it must include what I call the greater Bristol area, i.e. City of Bristol itself and the near neighbours, namely Kingswood, Warmley, Mangotsfield, Keynsham, Filton, Patchway and Long Ashton.
2. The age group – because we wanted to include all these places, it was decided we must limit those taking part to the over 70s. In fact, when all the demands of the over 70s had been met, we were able to extend the scope of some of the events to those over 65. We made allowance, of course, where the husband was over 70 and the wife was under 70.

3. Type of entertainment – we wanted to have some outdoor events for the more active people and some indoor events and we decided on three indoor and three outdoor types of entertainment. We also decided to limit everyone eligible to taking advantage of one outdoor and one indoor event. I will deal with the items of entertainment individually shortly.
4. The timing – we naturally wished to hold the Festival during a period when the weather was likely to be favourable but it was also necessary to hold it when we could get the best financial terms from the firms with whom we had to deal for entertainment, e.g. one of the forms of entertainment was coach outings and obviously the coach company could give us better terms out of the busy season. It was therefore decided that a week between Easter and Whitsuntide was the best period.

Other points to which we had to give attention were:

(a) Methods of making contact with those eligible to take part and
(b) The setting-up of an organisation for dealing with applications for the issuing of tickets. In this connection it was essential to establish a system which was fair to all and which guarded against abuse.

To turn first to the subject of the entertainment to be provided.

1. We took the Hippodrome Theatre for one week and laid on through Moss Empires an old time music hall show twice nightly which was able to cater for 1,500 at each house – a total of 18,000 people during the week. Such old-timers as Randolph Sutton (Bristol born), Hetty King and Marie Lloyd Junior were in the bill. This was

tremendously successful and all those people who attended entered into the spirit of the event with great enthusiasm. This cost £2,000.
2. We arranged coach outings during the week through Bristol Omnibus Company (who also had the assistance of coaches provided by Wessex Coaches and certain other firms) for 1,500 people a day going to seven different West Country resorts. Each person was also provided with a hot midday meal at a hotel or restaurant. The cost of this was approximately £7,500.
3. We chartered a Campbell Steamer for outings to Ilfracombe on two days of the week, taking 750 persons on each trip. Each person was provided with a packed lunch. Total cost including lunches was approximately £1,100.
4. We obtained the co-operation of Bristol cinemas to admit these old folk free, up to 5 p.m. daily, up to a total of 20,000 during the week.
5. We obtained the co-operation of Bristol Zoo to admit 20,000 during the week to the gardens.
6. Well known local artists provided a one night concert at the Colston Hall for which there were seats for 2,000.

This expended our total budget of £12,000. In fact, because the Bristol Zoo and Cinemas were very much under-bid, the final cost of the Festival was only £10,833.

I would like to make one or two comments about the above events in which I am supported by many who had close contact with the old folk.

(a) The Hippodrome might well be a one house show if we restrict those attending to the over 70s. They do not like going to the later house and this was a case where we threw the thing open to the over 65s, once the demands of the over 70s had been met.
(b) The Bristol Zoo and Cinemas were so poorly sup-

ported that I think we should discount them in the future, although we might well suggest to them that they could invite those eligible to take part in the Festival, to go free during that week. (The Zoo visits were very well supported the following year and were retained very successfully after that.)

(c) We should arrange half day coach outings as well as full day outings. Old people will not hesitate to go on long trips of any kind despite the fact in some cases it is not good for them, and therefore it is advisable there should be the opportunity for them to take shorter journeys.

There is no doubt the most popular things were the Hippodrome, coach outings and the steamer trips, and these should certainly be repeated.

It is strongly felt, in connection with the coach outings that it is quite unnecessary to give people the choice of seven different resorts. It is much better to tell individuals they can have an outing to a specific place and it is much easier to organise. They do not mind being told what to do but, if given a choice and one is unable to meet their first choice, they complain.

You will recall that I said there were some 35,000 over 70s in the area to be covered. Our indoor events would permit 40,000 people to take part and our outdoor events 30,000. But certain items of entertainment would cater for only as few as 2,000 (e.g. Colston Hall Concert) or 1,500 (Campbell Steamer Trips). One of my nightmares was that 20,000 people would ask to go on the Campbell Steamers and only 200 apply to go to the Zoo. Fortunately, although, as I have said, the Zoo and Cinemas were under-bid, none of the other events was ever over-bid. For instance, the coaches could have taken more people as also could the steamers and the Hippodrome, though not many more.

Having decided the area to be covered, the age

group, the date and the entertainment to be provided, there remained our two problems of making contact and setting up an organisation through which I could work.

We had, of course, the valuable medium of our own paper through which we could make known what people were required to do to take part in the Festival.

We could set up a big central booking office to which all those wishing to enjoy one of the forms of entertainment could make application if they were eligible. There were two major difficulties to this. Old people would have to travel to a central point which would be tiring and expensive, and the recording of everybody's application to try to avoid abuse and the donor's generosity through people applying to take part in more than their share would involve an impossible amount of clerical work. I decided, therefore, that the area must be split up into geographical regions and working committees established for each of these regions. Within the city boundary I took the municipal ward as a geographical unit and outside the boundary, the parish. I wrote to every councillor in these wards and parishes asking them to form the nucleus of a working committee which could invite sundry others to serve upon.

It is a great tribute to them that they worked as hard as they were requested to do.

They (a) canvassed the streets in their area and compiled a register of eligible old folk, inviting the old folk to make their bids for whatever entertainment they wished to take part in.

(b) informed me of the numbers eligible in their areas and applied to me for tickets for the entertainments requested. I allocated tickets accordingly and they

(c) undertook the delivery of all those tickets.

Each committee had a nominated secretary to whom I addressed all correspondence and from whom I received all queries.

The system worked very well but there were two main difficulties. Firstly most of the secretaries had to work either from their homes or in a few cases on specially selected nights in community centres or church halls. In future, each should have a small advertised headquarters at which the old folk can reasonably be expected to go and register and ultimately collect their tickets. The second difficulty was that the councillors were the main workers and our Festival fell at a time when they were intensely busy with the municipal election campaign. If the councillors are to be the main working members of our committees in the future we must avoid the work falling during the election period.

We have, however, had a firm offer from the Federation of Old Age Pension Associations, saying that many of their members would be willing on future occasions to take a much more active part at this committee level and to man these regional offices, which I think should be established within a period of three weeks prior to the Festival Week.

There were, of course, bound to be a large number of old people physically unfit to take advantage of the Festival. Obviously we had to do something for them. We decided to have a host and hostess for the Festival Week and invited Wilfred Pickles and his wife to fill this role. I would say here that they did their task admirably and contrary to rumour which I hope we effectively killed, they received no financial reward whatever. The *Evening Post* paid their travel expenses and for their entertainment and the Grand Hotel generously made no charge for their week's accommodation. So they were no cost to the Festival Fund whatever. It was to meet the case of these unfit people, that we used the services of Wilfred and Mabel Pickles mainly. I arranged a very exhaustive daily itinerary for them which involved visiting corporation, voluntary and private old folks' homes and also the personal homes of many old people who were brought to our notice as being unable to take part in active events. Even so, we felt at the end of the Festival, we did not cater sufficiently for those confined to their own homes; in future some sum of money should be set aside to buy small gifts for as many people as possible. I understand from those who have much greater experience of dealing with such cases that the main fact is that they should not feel they have been forgotten during such an event.

I see the future organisation on the following lines:

1. A central committee to provide ideas and, where possible, active helpers formed from, we hope, yourselves.
2. A paid organiser with an office and voluntary clerical aid. This I am fairly confident I can get from some of the more ardent workers of last May.
3. Area committees on a similar basis to those I have mentioned with a nominated secretary and a *publicly announced headquarters* in their respective area.

The paid organiser would work directly through the area committee secretary as I did and the old folks' applications and queries would be dealt with at the established offices to which I refer. I would point out that when it is decided what entertainment is to be provided next time, and as I have said the coaches, Hippodrome and steamers would be included, the paid organiser will have to make all the necessary contacts and arrangements with the firms concerned. The methods of ticket issue for the entertainments should be a subject for decision between the organiser and the firms but I do strongly recommend that this year the area secretaries make block bids for coaches for the people wanting to go on outings in their areas to specific places. This would cut out an area requesting, e.g. 8 seats for Weymouth, 110 for Sidmouth, 16 for Bournemouth, etc. and coach loads having to be compiled from 9,000 applications. The Bristol Omnibus Company who worked splendidly last time would prefer it this way and will, I know, give us excellent service'.

Colonel Harrison's meticulous planning had ensured the successful foundation of the Festival but, as he had indicated, there were inevitably difficulties with such a large scale event. 'The hour brought forth the man' in John James' appointment of the first paid Secretary, Major Alec Walker, known as 'Mick', who had just retired after nearly 40 years' service in the Army, 20 of them with the Glosters. A family man from Fishponds, he brought considerable management skill and enthusiasm to JJ's assistance. He was the architect, building energetically on his predecessor's ground plans, modifying and altering them where necessary.

His first task, with JJ's guidance was to assemble a strong committee, which consisted of an excellent Festival Chairman, Basil Stirratt, from a well known Bristol printers, Messrs, D.R. Moore, the Chairman of Round Table, S.B. 'Tiny' Lovering, Treasurer, joined by David Williams, Solicitor, A.C.N. Stubbs, D.R. Luke and K.A. 'Ken' Meyer, with his expertise in the theatrical world. Decisions were quickly made with less than four months' preparation available. 30,000 forms would be printed and a poster devised which later carried their guiding theme, 'The Old are Never Alone when Someone Remembers Them'. The experimental network committees under the chairmanship of local councillors would be discouraged to avoid any possibility of 'political bias'! The Festival, which JJ had originally thought, might be a 'one-off' celebration for 1963 only, would need to be extended for a longer period than one week. The age group to be served would be defined again as '70 and over', husband and wife qualifying provided either one was 70 years of age. Most important was the Committee's resolve to include all the housebound and infirm who had been unable to join in the fun.

There were an estimated number of 1750 housebound people in their own homes. Gift parcels were assembled for them containing a dozen or more items, tins of salmon, luncheon meat, rice pudding, cream, peaches, pears, fruit salad, packets of tea, self-raising flour, sugar, shortcake, chocolate and sweets. Another large group of the elderly housebound in hospitals, private and welfare homes were also to receive gifts. How were all these welcome parcels to be distributed? The Round Table came to the rescue. Their branches in and around Bristol took on the responsibility

Figure 30 With father looking forward to Festival night at the Bristol Hippodrome accompanied by Charles and Ann Fiddick. *(Bristol Evening Post)*

of collecting the seven tons of parcels from their tea chests stored in Maze Street, Barton Hill, and distributing them within ten days – a Herculean labour, cheerfully undertaken in the spirit engendered by the whole Festival enterprise. Many hands made light

In the gardens at Tower Court with daughter, Joan, wife, Margaret, and son-in-law, Clive.

Daughter Pat's grandson, Charles, helps great grandfather do his crossword, September, 1990.

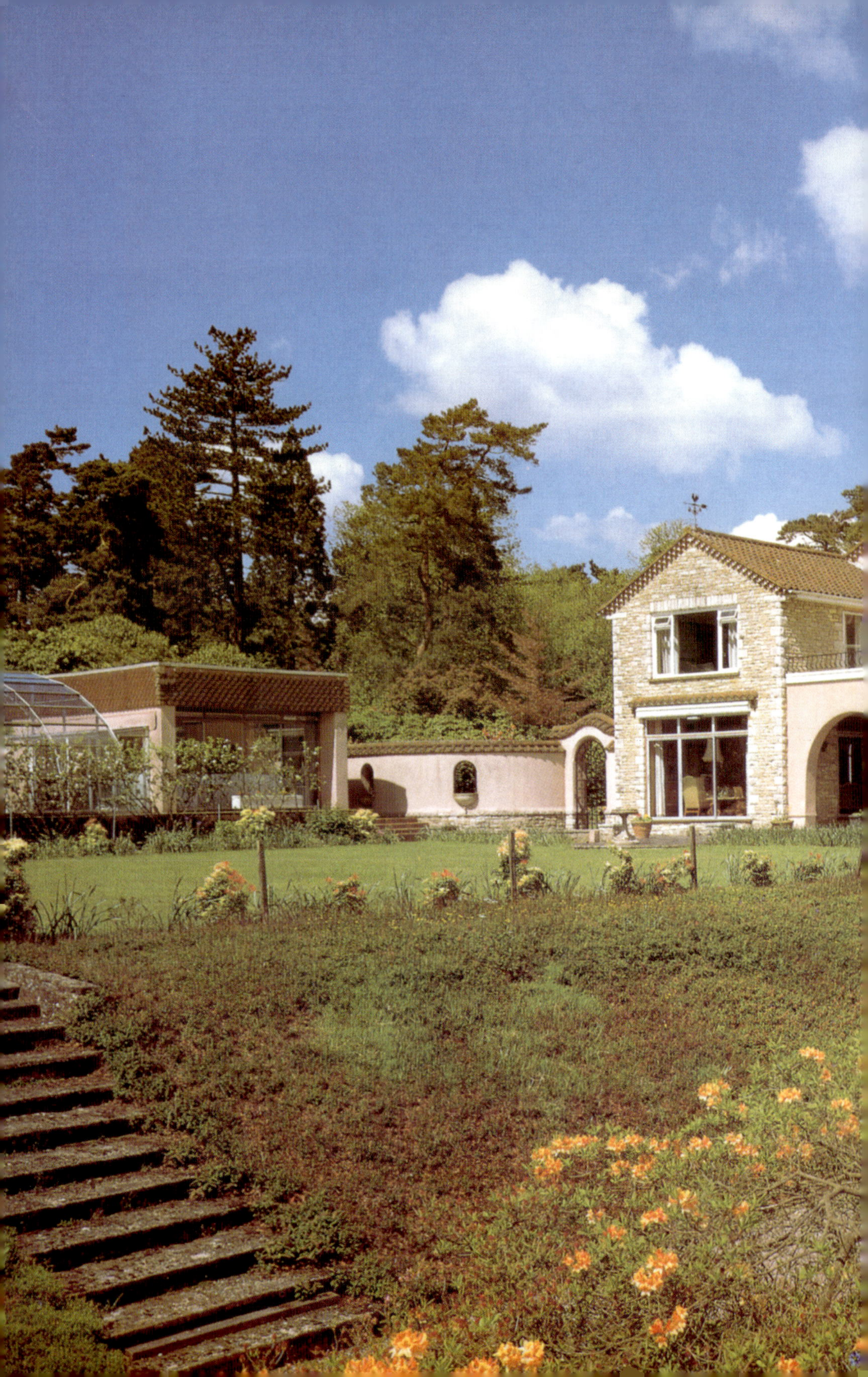

Tower Court,
Ascot, Berkshire
(Strutt & Parker)

With daughter, Joan, and grandchildren, Elizabeth and David, at Tower Court.

His favourite chair for work at Ascot.

The Making of a Philanthropist 1960–79

work. The Boys' Brigade, for example, were enlisted to deliver 6,700 tickets personally in 4,000 envelopes.

Major Walker's first Report delivered to JJ on 23 June, 1964, concluded with a huge list of thanks to the following:

> Bristol Round Table for their excellent work in and out of committee.
>
> *Bristol Evening Post* for their full coverage and Mr Harrison for his guidance and advice.
>
> The Director of the Bristol Zoological Gardens, the Council and their staff.
>
> Bristol Corporation Entertainment Committee and Mr Cowley (Colston Hall Entertainments Manager) and his staff. (The Festival was to return normally to the Hippodrome.)
>
> The Director of the Avon Boating Services Ltd. and their staff Mr Buckley, Traffic Manager, Mr Higgs, Tourist Manager and their staff of the Bristol Omnibus Company Ltd., Mr Smith-Cox, Managing Director of P. and A. Campbell Ltd. the Captain, Officers and Crew of the 'Bristol Queen' and all concerned.
>
> Bristol Civic Society and Mr Reece Winstone (lecturer on 'Bristol As It Is And As It Was')
>
> Mr Tolson, Director of A. J. Phippen Ltd and his staff for the gift food parcels.
>
> Mr Contannon of Coordination Traffic services and his staff for the storage, free of charge, of the gift food parcels.
>
> The Bristol Branch of the British Red Cross.
>
> The St John's Ambulance Brigade.
>
> The Youth Organisations.
>
> The Boys' Brigade Battalion of Bristol.
>
> The Good Companions' Service.

Figure 31 Waiting outside the Hippodrome. The First Festival 1963. *(Bristol Evening Post)*

The Women's Voluntary Service.

Mr Banner, Manager of Northcliffe House, and his staff.

The hundreds of individual helpers too numerous to mention by name, without whose help the Festival would not have been possible.

Further improvements were needed in planning, especially in the catering arrangements for substantial lunches and teas at various resorts. The general Committee verdict was that the Festival had been a success with the main objects achieved and that more old people had clearly benefited from an increased share in the arrangements. 'The team work has been terrific'. 'A special thank you to the personal staff of Mr John James for their advice and guidance, and to Mr Webb and his staff at Bridge House for willingness to produce the results on paper'.

Life was exhilarating for John James, concentrating hyperactively on his financial operations in Ascot and London but making time efficiently to join Mollie in Bristol. They took part with enjoyment and pride not only in the Festival, hosting the grand reception of the Music Hall stars and civic guests at the Hippodrome but also in countless visits to Old People's Homes, Church Halls, Lunch Clubs, community centres all over the city from Kingswood to Lawrence Weston. They took an unfeigned delight in pensioners' parties, stimulated donations to the *Evening Post*'s Christmas Appeals, and gave to the building of flats for old people. Mollie threw herself energetically into every mission of good will, being particularly proud also of becoming the first Chairman of the New Western Theatre Ballet, sponsoring their Charity Gala performance at the Theatre Royal.

The death of his daughter in April, 1964 was a hammer blow but the family rallied and resolved immediately and unanimously to found the Dawn James Trust, devoting her share of the family's wealth to charities centred on Bristol in her lasting memory. Though at first numbed with grief, they began with his guidance, to focus their concern and energies on further public service.

He was soon called into action not to support the elderly, but the pupils, staff and parents of Colston's Girls' School. A thriving voluntary aided secondary school with high academic standards and a flourishing community life it had been founded in 1891. The Education Authority sought in accordance with its wider plan for Bristol to convert it into a non selective neighbourhood school with entry at age 14. JJ, the experienced and strong swimmer, had no wish to be dragged into the whirlpool of educational politics, the comprehensives versus grammar schools controversy. The governors had voted for independence from the state system but more funds were essential if education there was to be open to girls from all social classes and neighbourhoods. His businessman's approach to the argument was characteristically direct, based on his simple principle. 'Always keep your eye on the ball! If you get into a rugby scrum there is always a lot of noise but the one thing that matters is the ball.' Colston's Girls' was a very good school. If the LEA proposals were put into effect it would be wrecked. 'I think someone has to make a stand'.

It was an added stimulus for him to act that the School had been funded by the Merchant Venturers' Society and that he had received his own education as a poor scholarship boy at the Merchant Venturers' Technical College. He and his family promised £100,000 without tying the governors' hands but hoping that this generous sum would be used to provide scholarships for girls whose ability qualified them for entry but whose parents could not afford the fees. The gift, given publicity in *The Times* and the national press was also intended to encourage other benefactors. 'I hope I shall be just one of the many people who will see that Colston's has no reason to fear'. The School's independence was secured. It was the first public sign he had given of a real interest in the cause of the young, a banner which he was to unfurl at the end of the next decade.

Year after year the Festival was gaining momentum and widespread popularity. May became the old people's month. Letters were sent to local churches inviting their prayers for the elderly on a designated Sunday in the month. City workers going to their offices at the Centre grew accustomed, some enviously, to seeing a fleet of crowded coaches on their way to favourite South and West coast resorts. The opening of the Severn Bridge made more excursions possible to Barry and Porthcawl, the Mayor of Barry coming every day to greet the visitors on their arrival. Very old age was clearly no barrier. The oldest recorded passenger was Mr Jimmy Wright in his 103rd year, accompanied by his daughter in law on their day out at Longleat in 1970. Two other centenarians, Mr Moody and Mrs Dumble, with her two septuagenarian daughters, travelled on the Four Counties and South Wales outings respectively in 1976 when over 100 guests were over 90 years of age. Experienced stewards were provided from the beginning in 1963 to accompany every coach to ensure passenger comfort. A short colour film was made reflecting the fun of those years.

Major Walker's small team was joined enthusiastically in 1970 by Mrs Gloria Powney, Bristol born and bred, returning from London to be based at Minster House. JJ had made the ground floor available for the Festival administration, involving recruitment of large temporary staff each year to cope with many thousands of letters of application, forms of registration, tickets, advertisements and posters for the post offices and other outlets, and communicating with hundreds of helpers.

The Making of a Philanthropist 1960–79

In its tenth year the Festival provided outings for nearly 20,000 people employing over 420 coach drivers. The records revealed that since it began over 150,000 pensioners had enjoyed free excursions, nearly 75,000 house-bound pensioners had received either a gift parcel or a voucher. The total cost was over £250,000. The organising committee were always accessible and open to ideas, suggestions or complaints, for not every aspect of such major undertaking could reach the same high standard. Basil Stirratt, the chairman, David Williams, vice-chairman, Ken Maggs and Graham Chamberlain were among those who gave sterling service. The support of the Round Table was outstanding. In 1974 for the first time a day conference was held for over 400 helpers, organised by Major Walker and Mrs Powney. Mollie James, who always went on the outings, spoke at the morning session stressing the vital role of the helpers in stewarding, providing first aid when necessary, on the tours and at the variety shows. The Committee was joined by two experienced members, David Dibben, a director of the John James Group and Trustee of the Dawn James Foundation, and Joan Wootten, an SRN and active helper from the birth of the Festival onwards.

The letters of thanks came in cascades to Minster House, short or prolix, grammatical or poorly spelt, in firm old-fashioned script or wavering hand, on Basildon Bond or paper from an exercise book, often humorous, sincere and moving. Some wrote in verse.

> '*On a coach trip*'
> Being one of those Senior Citizens
> On this beautiful morning in May
> With the sun shining what could be nicer
> Looking forward to an enjoyable day
>
> Our first stop – a café – near Bridgwater
> Where we adjourned for a 'Coffee Break'
> A chance to stretch our legs – or what have you?
> With may be closer friendships to make
>
> Then aboard through the morning to Dunster
> Where we enjoy together an excellent meal
> And even to those on a diet – poor souls!
> Little to belly-ache about – one feels!

To our coach again – our venue 'North Somerset
With scenery to gladden your eye
You can have your Costa Bravas or Majorcas
Give me an English Countryside – says I

Eventually arriving in Minehead
Filling the 'inner man' with a good tea
With an hour to spare sight-seeing
Or bathe your poor feet in the sea

Then homeward bound in the cool of the evening
The last stop at a Pub for a drink and a sing-song
With everyone happy and contented
All helping the evening along

Home at last – tired but grateful
For John James's generosity – 'full of cheer'
And some who have enjoyed our day out
If spared – may make the same trip next year

Yes! The Dawn James Annual Festival
Is a God-Send for 'old fogies' like me
Who unlike those who holiday abroad
Are not so well off as we would like to be.

                Anon, Old Age Pensioner of Clifton. 1977

Major Walker retired in 1978 in his sixteenth year as Secretary. He could look back on the staggering success of the Festival and the vast numbers participating. It was estimated that in one year the number of pensioners he had helped to visit Sidmouth on excursions was greater than the resort's entire population. The guest artists booked for the week at the Hippodrome had included household names in the Music Hall tradition, Arthur Askey, Elsie and Doris Waters, Sandy Powell, Tommy Trinder, Cyril Fletcher, Frankie Howerd, Morecambe and Wise, singers such as Ivor Emmanuel, musicians like Walter Landauer. There were spectacular productions with elaborate scenery and performing ponies. The performances on Saturday evenings were broadcast to hospital patients throughout the area and much appreciated. 'We must have a dinner at Foster's', wrote JJ in the margin of Alec Walker's final report.

    Mrs Powney took over the reins with some trepidation. Mr David

The Making of a Philanthropist 1960–79

Figure 32 'On the Prom' at Minehead 1963. *(Bristol Evening Post)*

Dibben, by then an experienced member of the committee took over the chairmanship. All future Festival arrangements were to be discussed with the immediate Dawn James Trustees and the old committee was wound up. Her first Report as Secretary in June 1979 ended, 'the Festival in general was trouble free and very successful. I am sure you will appreciate how relieved I am to be able to tell you this' 'SPLENDID!' commented JJ in the margin.

* * * *

His great concern was already being directed towards Bristol's historic schools and their fate. The tide of popular opinion was flowing strongly, if not irresistibly, towards the rapid national reorganisation of the maintained secondary schools. By 1974 some three-quarters of the schools in England and Wales had been reorganised on comprehensive lines. The newly elected Labour government announced that the supporting grant would be phased out from the country's 174 direct grant schools from September, 1976. The Butler Act of 1944 provided that direct grant schools had to fill their places with 25 per cent free scholarship pupils, who had attended elementary schools for at least two years, 25 per cent free reserved places were held at the disposal of the local Education Authority for pupils they nominated and whose fees they paid, and 50 per cent at the disposal of the school governors for fee payers or otherwise.

Bristol had seven direct grant schools. The Roman Catholic authorities with few exceptions joined the maintained system nationally. In Bristol, St Brendan's Boys' College was transformed into a large, coeducational, voluntary aided Sixth Form College and La Retraite Girls' School was regretfully closed. The five direct grant schools, Bristol Grammar School, the Cathedral School, Queen Elizabeth's Hospital, Redland High School and the Red Maids' School were facing a major crisis in the mid 1970s. Alarm bells were ringing in three areas – unprecedented soaring inflation, forecasts of a sharp decline in the secondary school population in the 1980s and, most important of all fundamentally, the fears that enforced independence would turn them into exclusive schools for the sons and daughters of the rich. Teachers and parents in all these schools were afraid that the country's educational system would become polarised between the small, high achieving private sector and the great majority of maintained schools. All five chose independence, albeit with considerable reluctance and anxiety at first.

John James was drawn irresistibly into this conflict of principles and practical problems. By birth and temperament he was instinctively sympathetic to both the traditional and independent approach. The nonconformist in him, that 'bit of a rebel' as he put it, propelled him into the fray. These famous schools were flourishing oaks in a fast changing educational landscape with roots strong and deep in the local community. They should not be axed.

He took the initiative in asking his colleague on the Old Folks' Committee, Mr David Williams, now Chairman of Governors of the Grammar School whether he could be of any use. He was not the man to throw money away sentimentally. He invited the Chairman and the author, then Headmaster, to meet him at Minster House. It was a crucial encounter. Both guests felt that they were representing not only their own school but all their friends in difficulty. JJ had clearly been impressed by those Old Bristolians with whom he had come into contact in business and by their regard for their school. He ran his finger up and down the school's accounts and financial forecasts like a concert pianist reading a fresh score, assimilating the details and implications with incredible rapidity. The questions came quietly and quickly. If the Chairman and the Head had been put into bat, JJ was the intimidating fast bowler, an amiable but astute player; Miss Pennington at his side was the umpire observing keenly the strengths and weaknesses of the participants and keeping the score too. 'What is your philosophy of education? Will it change because you are going independent? What is special about university education? How do you advise your pupils thinking about careers, especially in business and industry? Are Business Studies and Economics courses useful? Co-education? The role of parents? ... It was a searching, probing yet friendly examination and discussion.

JJ made his decision quickly. He authorised his first gift to Bristol Grammar School in the autumn of 1978 and soon followed this with similar gifts of £100,000 each to all the ex direct grant schools for bursaries or assisted places. 'I am just returning the bread upon the waters which someone once threw to me', referring to his scholarship to Merchant Venturers' Technical College. 'I am hoping that this money will help give boys and girls of similar backgrounds to my own the same start that I had. It's for the benefit of poor children in Bristol who cannot otherwise afford the fees'.

With further gifts to the already existing independent schools, Colston's Girls, Clifton High and Clifton College he was giving over a £1 million in this first round of benevolence. The author was to advise him shortly on the needs and the merits of Bristol's maintained schools and commended these to him when the opportunity arose. It gave him the greatest joy, pride and satisfaction now to be helping the young as well as the elderly. These were genuine rewards for him, though the local press was already beginning to comment on his modesty in March, 1979. 'Strangely there has been little public recognition offered to Mr James, a person who shuns publicity. But there must be thousands who would like to be associated with a public 'thank you' to him. What about it, Bristol?'

He dismissed such press talk from his mind. He was preoccupied with his negotiations for the sale of his companies to Wolseley Hughes. This accomplished, he would be freer to involve himself with the welfare of his native city. The precedents were good. His headquarters at Minster House were within a few hundred yards of distinguished predecessors in the city's history. Robert and Nicholas Thorne, merchant founders of the Tudor Grammar School had lived in Broad Street, John Carr, soap merchant, founder of Queen Elizabeth's Hospital, lived at 17 Baldwin Street opposite, Alderman John Whitson, merchant founder of Red Maids' School at 80 Nicholas Street, Edward Colston, baptised at Temple Church, had lived in Wine Street. In the 18th century the young Henry Wills, lived above his shop in Castle Street and set out daily by dog cart or on horseback with samples of snuff and tobacco for West Country villages and market towns. JJ might well have felt that he had joined the ranks and come of age as a Bristol philanthropist. He certainly judged that he was still fit at 73 and had so much to do.

7 'Let's Keep on Giving' – the High Tide of Benevolence 1979-94

1979 proved a watershed not only in the life of John James but also the country. Margaret Thatcher was elected prime minister in May. Crucial changes in the economy shaping the whole social climate took place as the 1970s gave way to the 1980s and her new government embarked on a decade of rigorous retrenchment and reform. New concepts and a revised vocabulary made their appearance for good or ill – monetarism, privatisation, streamlining heavy industries and downsizing work forces. Redundancies proliferated, rampant inflation was tamed, falling from the highly alarming peak of 27 per cent to 7.7 per cent in 1989. The government championed the pursuit of excellence, proclaimed the values of competition and individual initiative, stressing the supreme role of market forces and cost effectiveness in all enterprises. Inevitably there were increasingly severe pressures on the operations of the welfare state and on local authorities' role in social and educational services faced with rate capping. What greater need and opportunity for a philanthropist?

Liberated by the sale of his companies, John James now accelerated the pace and vastly extended the scope of his giving backed by his successful investments. He brought as much boundless energy, enthusiasm and enjoyment to giving away millions as he had in accumulating them. He kept his distance from political parties, never subscribing a penny to them, ever critical of high taxation, believing that he could use his own wealth more effectively than any government department. 'I prefer to be a-political', he said once, adding with characteristic provocation, 'I would like to be a 21st century communist. No one would be allowed to join my party unless they were putting more into the community chest than they were taking out of it. That's what we should aim for'. He was to return to this theme later.

He now moved swiftly to the aid of the comprehensive schools, offering £1 million and challenging 10 of them to raise up to £100,000 which he would match. The capital sum raised by the appeal and matching would be invested and only the interest thereon disbursed. Filton High School with 1400 pupils was the first to respond. Its Enrichment Fund to support worthwhile activities and develop the personal qualities of every pupil in their strong community impressed him greatly. Inflation was a running sore, eating away the assets needed to support residential experience for the pupils, assist needy children from poor families, encourage field work, sport and creative arts as well as provide goods and services for the benefit of all. An immediate example of the problem was the replacement of the vital school minibus used by two thirds of the pupils and staff. A gift from the Friends in 1976, it had cost over £2,900 then and more than £6,000 was required to replace it. JJ's offer triggered a splendid response from parents and well wishers. He wrote to the Headmaster, Mr Michael Smith, on Saturday November 17th 1979, 'I am so pleased that you and your associates have accepted my challenge and I do hope you will succeed on both scores. If you do, I shall be delighted to send you cheques totalling £100,000. By the way, if you do succeed in getting another £50,000 from your own resources, and £50,000 from 'outsiders' your capital fund will be £250,000 – a quarter of a million – what a splendid BEGINNING!'

It was a major breakthrough in state school funding. Filton's target being achieved within a few days of the deadline. 'I'm absolutely delighted', commented JJ. 'It'll give a spur to the other schools … the whole idea is to narrow the gap between the comprehensive schools and the public schools. It's also a way to get parents more involved. I'm the happiest man in Bristol. I send Filton my congratulations'. Enormous local enthusiasm had been aroused. JJ was happy to relate the story of the taxi driver parent who walked into the school office one morning, slapped down £25 on the desk and said, 'Tell James to match that!'

Other schools took up the challenge. Typical was Lockleaze on a large council housing estate where the Head had initial doubts

'Let's Keep on Giving'

about its ability to raise funds and an understandable reluctance to distort the school into a simple money-making institution. The parents there welcomed the opportunity to raise money for trips abroad, Outward Bound Courses, extra music lessons, sports coaching and special courses for promising pupils. Valiantly, they raised £13,500 in three years.

His generosity was spreading rapidly to every state school willing to accept it. They faced mounting financial problems as the decade developed and cuts in budgets proliferated. The Dawn James Trust, with Mrs Powney at the telephone and typewriter, was kept fully occupied with the mountainous financial and administrative detail involved for each individual school. Money for prizes, awards and subsidies for extra activities at the heads' discretion was willingly provided from 1981. In 1999 some 20 years after the start of the donations, the following schools were receiving gifts of £2,000 annually: Bedminster Down, Brislington, Filton High, Hartcliffe, Henbury, Lawrence Weston, Lockleaze, Monks Park, Patchway High, Portway Community, St Bernadette, St George Community, St Mary Redcliffe, St Thomas More, Speedwell, Withywood, Cotham Grammar, Fairfield Grammar, Hengrove, Pen Park, Whitefield Fishponds, Merrywood and Ashton Park.

He leapt into the unfamiliar world of education with great zest and curiosity to learn about this crucial area of Bristol's life. The Heads who met him at Minster House quickly found themselves caught up in a general knowledge quiz, philosophical questions and educational theories. A second massive gift of £1 million to the city's independent schools for their poorer scholars reflected his admiration and sympathy for parents, many of whom were making significant financial sacrifices to support their children.

His gifts brought him many new contacts and wider experiences. The boys at Clifton College which eventually received £490,000, mainly for bursaries, took part in a sponsored run to his house in Ascot, including his grandson, David, and swam in his pool. He returned the compliment later by opening their new swimming pool at the College. In November 1980 he was smuggled into Bristol Grammar School for a three hour morning visit away from the attentions of the press. His first call was an hour's session on his own with a lower sixth Economics set. He emerged having cheerfully identified the 'student of great promise', a girl who was later awarded a first in Economics and Business Management at the Oxford Polytechnic. He then faced a sixth form of 300 boys and girls, who questioned him on every subject under the sun. In conclusion they gave him the opportunity of declaring his belief in 'health, wealth and wisdom'. Tired but triumphant, he confessed quietly to the author, 'I wouldn't have your job for all the tea in China!' Afterwards he wrote 'You delighted me beyond measure by introducing me to such a wonderful group of sixth formers. They convinced me I should have struggled to get beyond the upper fifth. Your sixth form are a wonderful crowd with fascinating possibilities. Keep them "at it"! You have some great people there'. In 1982 when their 450th Birthday Appeal for £400,000 was flagging he kept the whole B.G.S. community 'at it' following his total surprise and unsolicited offer of a matching grant of £50,000. 'Never give up hope my boy!', he told the author. A community revitalised exceeded the target in three months. The dilapidated huts were demolished and the Princess Anne Building appeared at Tyndalls Park.

His initial thought in endowing awards had been to recognise the 'Victor Ludorum', the outstanding athlete or sportsman/woman in each school, a concept familiar to him from his RAF days in Malta, where Charles Fiddick had been outstanding. He very soon realised the immense variety of worthwhile projects and travel awards, which would set free the imagination, intelligence and altruism of the boys and girls judged worthy winners by the Heads.

Their initiatives amazed and fascinated him. The variety of projects undertaken by thousands of students was often breathtaking. Study and travel ranged from inland China to California, Thailand to Australia. Students embarked on a wide range of activities from butterfly collecting to furniture design and glacier exploration, or research into the comparative training for medical students in France and England. Community service inspired many, including one young man from Q.E.H., who used his award in the gap year between school and university to teach children in a Tibetan Buddhist monastery.

In October 1993, one of the students wrote to him,

'Dear Mr James,

At present I am in Israel enjoying the gorgeous weather. I have just heard the news about the scholarship and I am very grateful.

I thought you might be interested to hear what I am doing here. I'm spending four months on this kibbutz. The kibbutz is in the middle of the desert – I'm actually about 2 Km from the Jordan border. As regards Arab-Israeli relations, now is a very exciting time to be here. On the day that the treaty was signed I was sitting in a Bedouin tent with the rest of the group that I'm with. We are 40 leaders from the reform Jewish youth movements in England. The aim of the year is to learn about the issues which affect Israel and Judaism today and also to learn some leadership skills.

In February I will be going to Hawaii to an education centre as I could be involved in projects as varied as teaching English to new immigrants from Russia and Ethiopia, helping in the school's kindergarten, teaching programmes for Israeli youth or helping to run youth clubs in deprived areas. I will also be able to spend some time studying the issues relevant to today and also in improving my Hebrew.

If I don't become totally ensconced in Israeli society, I'll be returning to England next year to follow a course in chemical physics at Sheffield University.

Once again I wish to express my gratitude and hope I will be able to use your prize wisely'

Yours sincerely,

Rebecca Reese

Her benefactor wrote firmly at the top of her letter, 'VERY INTERESTING . JJ'

* * * *

At the start of the decade to add to his concern for the elderly and the young he helped launch a third mission, which was to aid the sick and the dying. His first major bid to help the hard-pressed National Health Service was decisive and dramatic, hailed in the nation's press, television and radio in March, 1980. The country had two heart transplant centres at Papworth, Cambridge, and Harefield, Uxbridge. Both hospitals were under-financed and unable to maintain their transplant programme. JJ's friend and rival in Radio Rentals, the millionaire David Robinson, came to the rescue of Papworth. JJ heard a powerful appeal for help for Harefield one evening a week later. By 11.30 a.m. the following morning, Friday 17th March, he had sent a promissory note for £300,000 to the hospital.

His action was very swift, but not impulsive. He was 'too canny' for that, as Don Hatwell, the *Evening Post*'s London editor reported. JJ had checked again on the authenticity of the broadcast, the reliability of the Hillingdon Health Authority and of its spokesman, a former *Bristol Evening Post* reporter. He met them both early that Friday morning, asking searching questions about transplants, surgeons and the qualities of both hospitals. He was pleased that a local trust had been set up to raise money. 'I like to help people who help themselves'. He had doubts briefly because, until then, his charitable giving had been centred on his home community. He was reassured to learn that patients from Bristol would go to Harefield, which was more accessible. The gift removed all financial anxiety for at least three years from the distinguished surgical team led by Mr Magdi Yacoub, who had been very tempted to move to the USA with its great medical resources. It ended the rumours and worries that the government were thinking of closing down Papworth. Remembering his daughter Dawn's death, he said, 'I know that if transplant surgery had been available then, she and I would have wanted to donate her heart'. He counted it a privilege to help the devoted specialists who were national assets. 'They have every right to be allowed to stay in business and I am lucky enough to be able to help them'. He added, 'I see this as a gift from Bristol to the capital'.

A second major gift to London came the following year. He was now spending his winters in Florida with Margaret but, as always, maintaining the closest daily contacts with home. They had moved their winter quarters immediately from Jamaica to Breakers' Row, Palm Beach after an intruder had been discovered in their house, Rio Chico. News came via the BBC that babies were dying because Westminster Hospital's bone marrow unit lacked funds necessary to carry out all the operations it wished. Professor Hobbs, the head of the unit, hailed the generous gift of £100,000, 'ending heartbreaking decisions about who should live and who should die'. Westminster could now double the number of patients treated. The Prime Minister expressed her delight at this 'wonderful gesture' and set up a commission to study the possibility of setting up more bone marrow transplant units in the country.

It was also becoming clear that extra voluntary effort was needed to provide more nursing care for those who were permanently incapacitated in their last years and for whom an old people's home was inadequate and inappropriate. The predominant terminal illness was cancer, most common in old age but also attacking the young. Dr. Cicely Saunders (later Dame) was a pioneer in the field with St. Christopher's Hospice in Sydenham. Bristol Merchant Venturers initiated a feasibility study under its former master, Mr Jack Britton, a friend of John James, in 1967, for a centre for the accommodation and care of the terminally ill. These early efforts were dogged by misfortunes and disappointment – the death of Professor A.V. Neale, Professor of Child Health at the university, whose Vice Chancellor, Sir Alec Merrison, proved a strong supporter – the financial cuts in the NHS – the resistance of authorities, doctors and nurses to the idea that a Hospice could provide a service of value to their patients, which they were not providing themselves. Under the overall chairmanship of Mr A. M. Urquhart assisted by Mrs Joan Bourns' supporting 'Friends of St Peter's Hospice', the Hospice for 'sharing the caring' was born at St. Peter's Lodge, in the family house and gardens of the Convent of the Sisters of Charity at Knowle. The first patient was admitted in May, 1980 to the centre which began with seven patients in three wards.

Huge funds were essential. The freehold had to be purchased; the Lodge had to be converted and imaginatively developed. The work of the home care nurses covering Bristol north and south had to be expanded to meet the growing appeals for help.

John James was immediately concerned and brought his sympathy and resolution to a cause of great compassion, which gradually won the heartfelt support and admiration of all Bristol. In 1980 he offered £500,000 phased over five years, readily postponed by him when there were problems in the third year, and resumed for the remaining period. At the same time he and his family joined energetically and enthusiastically in all the humbler day-to-day tasks of raising money led by the Friends. Large sums such as £1,000 were given for raffle prizes; he gave fund raising dinners, attended dances and social events, and urged that all supporters should have 'St Peter's Hospice Sharing the Caring' stickers on their cars. He took an active interest in all the details. His first wife Mollie was a guest speaker at many small group meetings and did patchwork for sales. Margaret was similarly engaged, adapting old eiderdowns to make pillows. In a thousand enterprises as well as major individual donations Sir Alec Merrison's Appeal Committee reached their target of £500,000. St Peter's Hospice new building was officially declared open by their Patron, the Duchess of Kent, on 24th October 1986.

The 'thank you' card sent out by the Hospice to all Friends and Supporters was a poem.

> The Tree of Light.
> Were a star quenched on high
> For ages would its light,
> Still travelling downwards from the sky
> Shine on our mortal night.
> So when a good man dies,
> For years beyond our ken
> The light he leaves behind him
> Shines upon the paths of men.

* * * *

The way of the philanthropist was not smooth or simple. Hard, sometimes unpopular, decisions had to be taken. His heart was still devoted to the old folk's Festival but society was changing and circumstances had altered rapidly since it began 20 years earlier. Miss Pennington had to write a difficult letter to the manager of the Hippodrome in October 1980. The Trust had decided after serious thought to discontinue the annual entertainment there, although the variety shows had been most enjoyable. The first reason was transport. The old people could be picked up more easily for their outings from points all over the city but they were finding it increasingly difficult to travel to and from the Centre for the show. The cost of public transport had risen 'ridiculously'. If they chose to attend one of the matinees they emerged into the growing volume of Bristol's dangerous rush hour traffic. The second reason was a sad comment on an increasing hazard. It was no longer so safe for them to be on the Centre after dark and to make their own way from their bus stops to their homes. They were afraid of being 'mugged'. The final straw was the increasing cost of the whole Festival, owing to the oil crisis, the rising petrol prices and the cost of meals. The Trust felt it right to concentrate on keeping the standards of the very popular excursions. Another reason for the declining attendances at the Hippodrome was now the popularity of television and radio which, ironically, JJ had helped to bring into their homes.

Another change took place in 1983 when the Trust decided to issue coach travel vouchers to all the pensioners wishing to go on an outing. The advantages were simply stated. 'You can travel on the date you choose. You can choose the tour you want. The tours will be available for you over a longer period. You can travel with eligible relatives or friends. You have a more varied programme. Clubs and groups can arrange to travel all together'. The original timing of the Festival was a period when many pensioners now had the opportunity of taking special 'out of season' holidays. When dates clashed it was not always easy to exchange tickets. The main difficulty had become the securing of hotels and restaurants with the appropriate facilities and space to cater for large parties at an agreed price and provide for travellers with special needs. 'Regretfully you will have to make your own arrangements covering meals'. This proved no discouragement to the thousands of appreciative pensioners who continued to enjoy outings to a greater area than ever of the South West and South Wales until the mid 1990s.

Gifts to help the attack on illness and major disease continued apace and became almost too numerous to mention or record. In

December, 1983 the Trust came to the aid of the Bristol and Avon Stroke Foundation to help victims and assist research. Although strokes were the third most common cause of death in the western world less than £50,000 was being spent on research here, compared with £5 million on heart disease and £30 million on cancer. The appeal director was hoping that local industrial and commercial companies would be sponsors. The Dawn James Trustees pledged £100,000 as soon as the appeal reached £250,000, which it achieved the following year. In March 1985 they promised £272,000 to keep the open heart unit at Guy's Hospital, London, so that 180 patients on the waiting list would have the chance of a life-saving operation. Interviewed from Florida by the BBC JJ said, 'it seemed that here was a hospital waiting to do something that people badly needed and all it wanted was money – so I thought I would do something about it. The NHS. can't afford it at the moment. It's up to us wealthy people to step in when the Government is unable to help ... at my age anything to do with the heart interests me, if you had the money, wouldn't you give it?'

In November, 1985 he pledged a massive donation of £1 million to buy a magnetic resonance imaging machine for the whole Bristol community based at Frenchay Hospital, Bristol. There were only eight MRI machines in the country; patients in the southwest were rarely able to benefit from them. The MRI was crucial in pinpointing cancers early with a remarkable degree of clarity. It was a magnificent gift which would put the Frenchay Hospital at the forefront of new medical technology. An appeal was made to local businesses to raise £500,000 to house the new machine, which was opened on 4th October, 1988 and treated over 1,000 patients in the first seven months.

At the same time the Trust on his initiative was giving generously towards the £250,000 leukaemia centre needed for adult patients at Southmead Hospital. Three years later he answered the appeal from Southmead with another million pounds to buy a shock-wave lithotripsy machine. This new high technology shattered kidney and gall stones, using ultrasonic shock waves. German medical researchers in 1980 required 4 days to produce the required shock waves; Southmead's machine produced two a minute. Patients were now needing to spend only a day or two in hospital instead of a week or more. There were only two lithotripters in the country at London and Manchester treating 15–16 patients a week. Mr Feneley, the well known consultant urologist, hailed optimistically this fine donation to a unit which had started on a shoestring. 'The advances are so exciting. We must get rid of this doom and gloom attitude to the Health Service'. The cost of maintenance was high, £160,000 a year. JJ's gift instigated a multitude of fund raising efforts, large and small, starting on June 18th when staff in the urology department exuberantly pushed beds, minus patients, from the hospital grounds via Gloucester Road to the city docks.

'Let's keep on giving', said John James reflecting the fervour of the day.

Causes great and small, the more personal the better, occupied his working time and spurred him on to yet more effort to make money by prudent investment and trading in stocks and shares. Visitors to his home at Ascot might well be interrupted by phone calls after which he would report with a smile of satisfaction 'that's another x thousand for the Trust'. This was not 'hard work' for him; he disliked the term, preferring 'the efficient use of time'. He could achieve, rarely lose, a five figure sum by telephone between lunch and tea but he kept strictly to his daily routine, 30 lengths in his pool at breakfast time, a lunch, a siesta at sometime during the afternoon, another half a mile swim in the early evening. After dinner, more substantial, with champagne rather than wine, came chess or cards, lengthy and probing discussions with guests or a quiet game of backgammon with Margaret for the housekeeping money. 'I'm catching up on him and he doesn't like it', she alleged. His thrift was exemplary. He was delighted at the laughter, in which he readily shared, when opening the new Frenchay Hospital scanner by cutting the thick blue ribbon at one side only, not at the centre, so that it could be rolled up and used again.

* * * *

He never sought honours but they came gradually to him in the 1980s; some formal recognition was also denied him. In the New

Years Honours List for 1981 he was awarded the CBE for his services to charity. 'The kindest millionaire', said the *Sun*, 'the West's Mr Bountiful', added the *Western Daily Press*. 'Mr Charity is a CBE' announced the *Bristol Evening Post*. On his winter holiday across the Atlantic JJ expressed his pleasure.

He was even more delighted in July 1983 to receive the Honorary Degree of Doctor of Laws from the University of Bristol. He looked very smart and fit in his scarlet degree robes. 'I loved the occasion' he said, adding with a characteristically wry smile that he wondered how much it had cost to hold such a ceremony. It was a very grand occasion in the packed and colourful Great Hall. The Orator, Professor Buller, began his tribute, 'Mr Vice-Chancellor, John James, who stands before you, is at heart a shy man who does not enjoy public occasions. Indeed it is my belief that, had it been proper for this university to grant him an Honorary Degree in absentia, John James might have preferred to avoid the public gaze. But such action would not have been appropriate and consequently, for a brief period, his shyness bows to protocol.' Outlining his startling story of business acumen and success he declared, 'laudatory though the creation of wealth may be, this University seeks to honour John James today not because he made money and in so doing has created many jobs and opportunities for others, but also because of the use to which he has put much of that wealth … today at the age of 77 he lives for most of the time he spends in this country at his home in Ascot but he retains a flat in Bristol (by the Sea Walls), which he visits regularly. He looks forward to the day when the Dawn James Foundation has yet more capital, which will enable it to make even more generous gifts to deserving causes for many years to come'.

'Mr Vice Chancellor, the City of Bristol and this University is rightly proud of John James, millionaire and philanthropist. I present to you John James as eminently worthy of the degree of Doctor of Laws, *honoris causa*'. Thunderous applause greeted him from the pillars of academe in their distinguished robes behind him on the platform and the hundreds of young students and parents in front of him. Did he recall those early struggles of his life in Philip Street, Bedminster, the Headmaster's letter to his father, urging him to keep John at school eventually to try for a coveted university place? He was clearly moved.

1986, the year of his 80th birthday found him more mellow but as mentally active and optimistic as ever. Health came first. 'What's the world to a man if his wife is a widow?' He was raising his sights. He asked for ideas on how funds for Bristol ought to be allocated in percentage terms. If people had £100 to spend, what proportion would they spend on different community needs?

There was a torrent of replies. It could be a blueprint for a utopian Bristol perhaps but behind the publicity and all the passionate debate which he instigated lay the cherished, long-held vision of a community chest for Bristol. As early as 1970 when he was approached to help the renowned Theatre Royal out of its sadly periodic difficulties he had stated his private views trenchantly in public. 'Bristolians should be looking not to '70s or '80s but to the 21st century', he told the drama critic, John Coe. A new body should be formed to succeed the current appeal committee with three different sets of people – the artists like the artistic director, the local creators of wealth and people like the University vice chancellor to hold the balance. Using the Dawn James Trust created five years earlier as an example, which had achieved £100,000 a year in income, he urged Bristolians to establish a community chest with a capital fund of £100 million, which, properly invested would provide an income of £6 million a year to help finance not only the Bristol Old Vic but many other very worthwhile causes. The Old Folks' Festival had been an invaluable experience for deploying funds but now was surely the time to plan ahead. He made some incisively challenging remarks, urged the other rich people in society to part with more of their money and to join together to explain fully to the people what an exciting opportunity this could be.

His views of 1970 and earlier were strongly reinforced for him by the American experience researched in W. A Nielsen's book *The Golden Donors*, which he read avidly, listing 30 pages for special notes. It was an analysis of the people, policies and performance of the 36 largest financial foundations in the USA including the Fords and Rockefellers. JJ was deeply interested in the story of the pioneering Cleveland Community Foundation in Ohio, begun in 1914. A responsible group of leading citizens in the city, a little larger than Bristol, in partnership with the trustee banks aimed to provide unified management for a number of charitable trusts and to encourage donations and endowments. JJ underlined with his pen the report that the city's bankers initially held back, 'being sceptical about the new fangled, over idealistic and tricky concept', though blessings had been pronounced by Andrew Carnegie and John D Rockefeller and the idea was to be copied in many cities.

The Cleveland bankers commissioned surveys of their most pressing, municipal problems, welfare for the unemployed, the schools system, the recreational facilities etc. By 1917 a full time Director was appointed, Raymond Moley, who was later to join President Franklin D Roosevelt's 'brains trust' for the New Deal with its 'pump priming' approach to welfare, which JJ used. A general upsurge in philanthropic giving, aided by changes in tax law in the 1960s led to a further growth in trust finances. By 1985 the Cleveland Foundation with approximately $260 million (approx. £150 million), New York $370 million, San Francisco $400 million were able to make annual charitable grants of 6–8 per cent of their income, giving substantial support to health, social services, education, the arts and the revitalisation of neighbourhoods. JJ knew well the differences between American and British societies and history, and realised that his question was simplistic; inwardly he could not help feeling, 'if Cleveland can do it, why not Bristol? If the wealthy citizens of Cleveland could contribute generously to the community chest, why not Bristol's?' He sympathised with Roosevelt's declaration in a different context, 'the only thing we have to fear is fear itself'.

The letters were now cascading into the offices of the local press plus personal letters to Downing Street, urging that further recognition should be given him, both local and national. On October 14, 1986 the Liberal councillor of the Easton Ward asked that the city council should consider bestowing the honorary freedom of the city on Mr John James. This was supported by the Conservative group leader who wished to see it win all-party support. The leader of the Labour majority said 'I am sure that Mr James' gifts were not given with the aim of receiving an honour. I am sure that Mr

James would recognise that many citizens made generous gifts to the city, according to their own ability and circumstances. I am sure he would consider bestowing the freedom of the City to be unfair, when other people also make contributions, both great and small'. The discussion in committee was shadowed by parochialism, the party politics of ideologies and envy. An imaginative and popular suggestion was buried in the Policy and Resources Committee before it could be taken to the whole council. The proposers, understandably unwilling to embarrass him further, did not raise the matter again. The letters to the local press expressed indignation and disappointment. 'I expect Mr James has upset a lot of Bristolians. Does Councillor Robertson know that for the last three years thousands of us have been trying to get Mr James honoured for all the joy and help he has given to many of us?'

* * * *

Greater magnanimity and appreciation were to come from a very different quarter. The historic Merchant Venturers' Society established by Edward VI in 1552 wielded the greatest influence in Bristol's charitable ventures. Its motto 'Indocilis Pauperiem Pati', 'untaught to endure poverty', was very appropriate. It could apply both to individuals who were not prepared to tolerate personal poverty or to the united philanthropic endeavours of the society. Its official historian, Professor Patrick McGrath, wrote that there was no such thing as a typical Merchant Venturer but certain characteristics stood out in the 1970s. 'The majority attended public schools and a considerable proportion are Oxbridge graduates. Many served with distinction in the army or navy in one or other, sometimes both world wars ... most appear to be Conservative in politics and Church of England in religion. Many are making major contributions to voluntary public service of all kinds'. Their business interests were varied, some held the highest executive and managerial positions in large-scale enterprises in and around Bristol. This was no milieu in which John James could readily feel comfortable and at ease. He had been critical of its oligarchic nature and had stressed the need for a new approach to charitable enterprises by local businessmen. He was never a 'good club man', always the swift fly half, who kept at a distance from the Old Boys' scrums.

The Society had been well aware at times of its problems throughout the century, undergoing reappraisals from the beginning of the welfare state pre-1914 when its radical treasurer, W W Ward, saw it in grave danger of becoming a complacent anachronism, which had served its purpose. Critical members stressed swifter undertaking of new forms of service to the post-1945 society with its National Health Service and full blown welfare state. Periods of relative inertia alternated with urgent self scrutiny. John James was too outstanding and critical an individualist to be brought easily on board the great ship, Merchant Venturer, Charles Clarke, a former Master of the Society, said of him in his memorial service tribute, 'internal foolishness prevented a proposal that he should become a member when his cause was taken up enthusiastically by the wrong person'.

Wiser and more perceptive counsel prevailed with the passage of time. In 1986 a celebratory Dinner for him was followed by a letter from the Master, Sir John Wills. 'It has long been the custom to grant Honorary Membership to persons of exceptional national distinction and our two present Honorary members are his Royal Highness, the Duke of Edinburgh and His Royal Highness the Prince of Wales. In former years it was quite usual to invite to honorary membership those who had rendered particular service to the city. No such appointment has been made since 1931 ...' He urged him to accept his invitation on behalf of all members recognising 'your quite exceptional generosity to the City'.

The unanimous election greeted with acclaim in the Great Hall on The Promenade in Clifton was followed by an invitation to John and Margaret to the ceremony on Friday, 24 April, 1987. At the top of the letter JJ wrote in capitals. 'RECEIVED 11.2.87. WE'LL BE THERE'.

The Master, Mr George McWatters, gave his good humoured speech of welcome to 'a Bristolian, born and bred', 'a very well disciplined man', an admirer of the American comedian, Jack Benny and a man who motivated charity by helping other people to help themselves and inspired others to achieve a success they might never have thought of. He praised his foresight. 'I remember you chiding me and saying many years ago that the role of the Society of Merchant Venturers needed a new approach. You will be pleased to learn that this is happening and we are at this moment actively promoting the establishment of the Greater Bristol Trust – a trust to look after the needs of the young and the elderly and to promote employment within the city. We are also seeking means to extend the membership of our Society'.

'We believe that this Society should continue to act as it has in the past and be a catalyst, or indeed a trustee of funds in the future development of Bristol. It is not true that private generosity can no longer do in Britain for its cities, for our arts, for our education and for our health what it does in America. We believe in the Greater Bristol Trust'. It was a ringing optimistic, if tardy vindication of John James' vision. In 1999 the Greater Bristol Trust, whose Chairman was the Vice Chancellor of the University of the West of England, held funds of £5 million, initially underwritten by the Merchant Venturers and chaired by Sir John Wills. It received donations of well over £1 million, double those of the previous year, providing 'a vehicle for Bristolians to put something back into their community'. The funding was an extremely long way short of JJ's target but its operations reflected his hope with its priority to the young, its Impact Programme, the Southmead Project, which attracted national attention as a new way of tackling drug abuse on a council estate.

A month after the ceremony in the Merchants' Hall he was invited to become the first honorary member of the recently formed Guild of Guardians. This was formed to support the Mansion House, which there had been talk of selling, and to assist the Lord Mayor in the performance of his or her civic duties. In addition to developing the amenities of the Mansion House, such as the glassware, the silverware and furniture, and landscaping the driveway, the Guild sponsored new lighting in the Lord Mayor's Chapel, and supported the Clifton Suspension Bridge Look Out. One of their most unusual projects was the reintroduction of an extra minute hand on the Corn Exchange clock to signify that before 1841 Bristol had its own time which was 11 minutes ahead of Greenwich Mean Time. He was intrigued and delighted to accept the honour from the Guardians, representing over 40 companies as well as individuals.

The tide of giving continued to flow at speed reinforced by his skilful, experienced play in the preference shares market, which earned a return of 29 per cent over six years. He told the *Financial Times*, 'Preference shareholders have had a rough time in the past. Boards tend to say "they don't have a vote, we can ignore them". But I don't see why lackadaisical boards should get away with it. We can do more good with the money we make than some of the Boards of companies do for their shareholders'. The appeals for help flooded in to Ascot and Minster House. He and his wife opened and read them diligently as did Miss Pennington and Mrs Powney in Bristol. He was pleased to give another huge, six figure sum, for example, to Southmead Hospital to purchase an ultra sound scanner for the ante-natal clinic but derived great pleasure too from his gifts to deserving individuals or smaller groups – to the young daughter of a single parent urgently needing money for music lessons, the veterans of the 1944 Normandy Campaign, to soldiers of 70 and over to attend the annual Coldstream Guards Dinner locally, to provide tickets to veterans and families for the annual Festival of Remembrance at the Colston Hall, and to flats for British Legion members, the John James Court at Lockleaze. The gifts seemed infinite. 'I feel like a fireman coming to the rescue at times', he confessed privately. A special personal happiness was his financial support to schools for the new book of swimming instruction written by the swimming instructor, Len Shearn, who had taught his daughter, Dawn. The foreword was written by Bristolian Olympic skater, Robin Cousins.

Of the thousands of gifts one was very close to his heart. It was relatively small, though the Trust increased it more than a hundred fold after his death, but sentimental and symbolic. Chris Ducker, an *Evening Post* reporter, revealed the details after JJ's death.

David Beasant, a retired taxi driver, fought for the creation of Windmill Hill City Farm. There was much enthusiasm but no money to build the Farm in an area that was just a rubbish tip, earmarked for a road that was never built. 'I knew Mr James', said David, 'I used to give him a lift in my cab – while my wife, Marie used to serve him lunch as a waitress in King Arthur's

Kitchen, the former Broadmead café. As we were well aware he had a few bob and strong local connections we wrote asking him for a meeting. Within a few days we had been invited to his office in Baldwin Street and we were explaining what the farm idea was all about. Mr James asked numerous questions – he was no "mug" of course when it came to money – before reaching for his cheque book. He gave us £2,000, a tremendous sum then (1976) with a promise of another £1,000 in each of the first ten years. Typically he insisted that there must be no publicity about the gift. And there was another condition – that each year we delivered to him a cabbage grown on the very spot where his home once stood. That's something I did until Mr James began to suffer poor health at the end of his life.'

Windmill Hill City farm became an inspiration stimulating further gifts from local companies, trusts and individuals. It provided fun and education for children, some 400 a day in summer holidays, became a meeting place for many local groups, including an 'age exchange' where young and old could meet and learn from each other and provided training programmes for unemployed youngsters. David Beasant remembered JJ's visits with his secretary. 'He was a Bristol South man through and through – blunt and to the point. There was no edge to him but his heart was in the right place…. He spent a happy time pointing out the building he used to climb as a kid and the tree where he pinched a few apples'. Some of the buildings were rightly named after him.

Gradually the passing years took their toll in bereavements and worsening health, so that more and more responsibilities were taken on by his very capable and loyal staff, pre-eminently still Miss Pennington and Mrs Powney. His second wife, Margaret, a very loyal companion in 19 years of marriage died in 1991. Mollie, who still took an active part to the end in the Old Folks Festival and other charities, died the following year.

He was 88 years old. After a stay in hospital in Slough necessitating the replacement of a painful broken hip, he made his major decision, welcomed by the family, to leave Tower Court, Ascot in 1994. The Bristol flier had climbed to the stratosphere on an adventure beyond his wildest imaginings. Now it was time to come home for good.

8 The End of a Life 1994–96: The End of the Century

'Growing old is acceptable, provided you grow into it graciously', John James once told his grandson, David. The sterling example of his own father was always before him. He had constantly thought of spending his final years in the city of his birth with its stirring history.

> '   a street of masts
> And pennants from all nations of the earth,
> Streaming below the houses, piled aloft
> Hill above hill ......'
>
>   wrote William Bowler in 1829.

John Betjeman, born in the same year, 1906, as JJ from a very different social background, always praised the great character and quality of this special place by the Avon.

> 'Then all Somerset was round me
> and I saw the clippers ride,
> High above the moonlit houses
> triple masted on the tide
> By the tall embattled church towers
> of the Bristol waterside'.

The landscape of Bristol was deeply etched in his mind. He needed no promptings from romantic poets. Despite all the depredation of post-war building developers the heartbeat of 'his' city was as strong for him as ever and he was determined to be back.

But where was such a private, at times very reclusive man to live? His daughter, Joan, spent many months searching and negotiating, often fruitlessly, before finding the most agreeable home for him. It was a large penthouse flat, on the edge of the Downs, over 400 acres of beautiful common land, grass and trees to be enjoyed in perpetuity by the citizens of Bristol, under the supervision of the council and Merchant Venturers' Society. From the extensive windows on the balcony he could enjoy wonderful views of the Bristol Channel, the hills on the Welsh coast and the patchwork of Bristol's roofs, houses, streets and parks. Vital also for him was the presence of his sister Ann, in a neighbouring block of flats, to whom he would look across and wave each day.

He moved shortly before his 88th birthday. His faithful housekeepers, Bill and Jean, came with him from Tower Court and were found accommodation nearby. He loved to walk with his stick, accompanied by family or friends across the Downs through the changing seasons to the Sea Walls, gazing at the Suspension Bridge over the river and down to the sea. The view was so different from his Bedminster days on the other side of the river. Joan drove him around the city to look at old, familiar and also fast changing places from his childhood.

His approach to life was always positive and hopeful, sustained by a keen sense of humour, which ranged widely. He enjoyed the comic genius of Charlie Chaplin, whose autobiography he kept, the wit of Shaw and the engaging thrift of the American comedian, Jack Benny. He related his two favourite stories of the latter's meanness with huge relish. 'Your money or your life!', said the hold-up man. 'I'm thinking about it', said Benny. . . . 'You can't take it with you', said the moralist. 'Then I'm not going!', came the retort. JJ signalled his intentions in retirement immediately upon his arrival at Victoria Court, writing in capitals inside a book on business, 'WHATEVER YOU ARE AFTER, LET IT CONTAIN LAUGHTER. 8-8-94'.

One of his greatest pleasures was the contemplation of his pictures, which Joan arranged to be transported to his new apartment. There were far too many for the flat but they could be stored and brought out when he felt the need to change. This was an immense satisfaction to him. It was characteristic of him to avoid the glare of publicity and the major auctions of Sothebys or Christies, the fight to acquire any of the world's most famous paintings at exorbitant prices.

His enthusiasm for art led him to several London dealers, one

Party time in Honolulu, January 1961, for sisters Dawn *(right)*, and Joan *(left)*.

Mollie fundraising for the scanner at Frenchay Hospital.

JJ outside the Royal Fort Lecture Theatre with the author after his Question and Answer session with 300 sixth formers, November 1980.

The house in the West Indies, *Rio Chico.*

John James CBE a proud day at Buckingham Palace with Margaret and Joan – 1981. *(K.R. Bray Photography)*

Doctors of Laws, the University of Bristol, in the Great Hall, July 1983. *(University of Bristol Arts Faculty Photographic Unit)*

With Joan at Breakers Row, Florida. 1983.

Backgammon with Margaret at Breakers Row, Florida.

MERCHANTS' HALL, BRISTOL

24th April, 1987

Be it remembered that on this day

John James C.B.E.

was admitted as a Member of The Incorporated Society of Merchant Venturers of the City of Bristol.

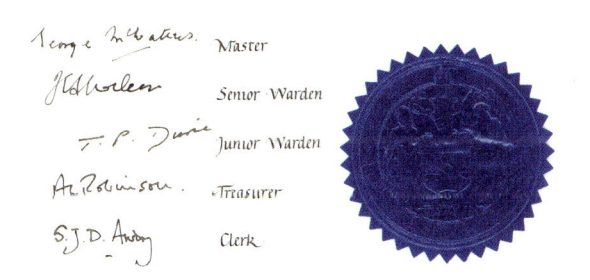

George McGaters. — Master
J.A. Worlean — Senior Warden
T. P. Davie — Junior Warden
A. Robinson — Treasurer
S.J.D. Awdry — Clerk

Certificate of admittance as a member of The Incorporated Society of Merchant Venturers.

With Margaret at the Trust Headquarters. 1990.

A keen battle of wits with grandson, David. *(Maureen Dunn)*

The End of a Life 1994–6: The End of the Century 121

of his principal agents being Maurice Furnell, Director of MacConnel-Mason in Duke Street, whose galleries had been established over a century earlier. He wrote in a full and revealing tribute, 'I can remember quite vividly the first time that Mr and Mrs James came into the galleries at St James's. We had in the window a small pair of Venetian paintings by a Peruvian nineteenth century artist, namely Frederico del Campo. They came into the Gallery to ask the price of the paintings and, at this stage, not realising who he was, I took him to be a passer-by making a casual enquiry. He asked if he could take the paintings to his home in Ascot.

Mr James purchased the pair of paintings and that first meeting twenty five years ago was the start of what I consider a very long relationship.

Mr and Mrs James would visit London perhaps two or three times during the year and would always stay at the Berkeley Hotel, and our gallery would become one of their main visiting points. Over the course of many years he formed a wonderful collection of English and European nineteenth century romantic paintings. Our gallery was by no means the first he ever visited but he was to become a major client.

I recall him telling me that the very first painting he purchased was soon after the second world war, which was a superb candle-lit market scene by the celebrated nineteenth century artist, Petrus van Schendel, and on one of my many visits to his home he showed me the back of the painting with the original asking price from the gallery where he purchased it, which was eighty guineas.

Even then he had a wonderful eye for quality and detail in paintings.

As a dealer I would always ask him what his favourite paintings were and his reply was. 'I love each and every one of them'. He had a series of paintings by one of the leading members of the Orientalist School. These paintings gave him tremendous pleasure and each time I visited his home it gave me a great deal of joy to examine the paintings closely and carefully and to admire the sheer quality and feeling in these figurative works.

The walls of his magnificent home in Ascot became full of some of the most beautiful nineteenth century paintings that one could see. To ascend the spiral staircase was a treat in itself. Above each tread of the stair hung a magnificent miniature oil painting depicting life in Europe in the late nineteenth century, paintings full of characters, colour and vibrancy, beautiful little paintings'.

The collection mirrored the many facets of the owner, his flair as a connoisseur, who made his judgements swiftly and instinctively without regard for 'artyness', the fickleness of popular taste. It was typical of him to 'adopt' an artist like Charles Spencelayh, an unfashionable and highly industrious artist, who painted unfashionable subjects from lower middle class life and was never made an RA, though his pictures were hung at the Academy for over 60 years. Spencelayh was the subject of a tribute in the *Sunday Times* in 1976 which praised the seriousness of his work beneath his odd diffidence and quirky sense of humour.

To the pleasure of his paintings was added the pleasure John James took in his books. Over the years he had amassed a fascinating and varied collection, companions whom he also brought with him. From the early days came his school prize, *A Gateway to Tennyson* followed by the books he needed in his urgent bid for self education. Pride of place among these went to Lancelot Hogben's ground-breaking *Mathematics for the Million*, published initially in 1936, the first of the Primers for the Age of Plenty, a hugely popular survey 'aiming to stimulate the interest and remove the inferiority complex of some of the Millions who have given up the hope of learning through the usual channels'. Chapters on 'Mathematics, the Mirror of Civilisation' and 'Statistics, the Arithmetic of Human Welfare' would have been especially significant for him. One shelf at Tower Court ranged from Kipling to O. Henry's *Short Stories*, Driberg's *Life of Beaverbrook*, *English Goldsmiths and their Marks* and *The History of the Merchant Venturers of Bristol*.

There were serious volumes in abundance on business, finance and management tempered by hilarious books puncturing the jargon, and the pomposity of the company world like *Great Commercial Disasters* ('This is a bloody business', William Shakespeare) or *How to Run a Bassoon Factory*. He took an early interest in cosmology, cybernetics, computerisation and environmental issues long before the term 'politically correct' came into view. His lighter reading included novels by H. E. Bates and adventure stories, true or fictional, especially of the RAF in both wars.

He found the experiences of other outstanding men of business related in their biographies and autobiographies of particular value. These ranged from great West Country philanthropists like the Wills family and Sir George White, and in Wales, Sir Julian Hodge, with whom he also corresponded, to Lord Nuffield and Sir John Cohen. He studied the transatlantic giants, the Fords, Gettys, Rockefellers and Carnegies. Their stories were often full of sound advice, their vicissitudes a constant reminder to him to keep on his toes at all times. Thinking of them, he felt that he had been mistaken in about 40 per cent of his decision making but was highly relieved that 60 per cent turned out so well. 'Sometimes I feel a complete clot', he said, 'but somehow I've always been able to drag myself back from the abyss. I do have the ability to succeed'.

Restraining him also from 'folie de grandeur' were authors like Shaw and A.J.P. Taylor, whose *English History 1914–45* came from as stimulating, at times infuriating, and controversial a personality as JJ himself, also born in 1906. He had lived through Taylor's history. The ex-squadron leader, whose native Bedminster had been blitzed, could readily identify with some of the historian's conclusions. 'In the Second World War the British people came of age. This was a people's war ... (they) had set out to destroy Hitler and National Socialism – 'Victory at all costs'. They succeeded. No English soldier who rode with the tanks into liberated Belgium or saw the German murder camps at Dacha or Buchenwald could doubt that the way had been a noble crusade. The British were the only people who went through both world wars from beginning to end, yet they remained a peaceful and civilised people, tolerant, patient and generous. Traditional values lost much of their force. Other values took their place. Imperial greatness was on the way out; the welfare state was on the way in. The British Empire declined; the condition of the people improved. Few now sang 'Land of Hope and Glory! Few even sang 'England Arise! England had risen all the same'.

His favourite author was undoubtedly George Bernard Shaw, the Irishman who became the greatest playwright in the English language in the first half of the twentieth century. JJ relished the rapier thrust of his wit, the brilliance and clarity of his ideas, his attack on humbug and traditional taboos, his championship of greater equality between the sexes and the classes, and his search for a meaning to life. He could not share all Shaw's subversive and negative criticisms but loved to 'converse' with him. This he sometimes did in the pages of Shaw's books, making notes of points he appreciated or resisted. 'Life is an adventure, not the compounding of a prescription. Money and sex have their place in life with all the other things.... If women had property they would either not marry or marry somebody else.... This also happens to men but less often as men are still <u>the economically self-sufficient sex</u>'. JJ underlined this and added two firm question marks.

He combed happily through the gems in Shaw's letters to Nancy Astor in 1929, agreeing from his own salutary experience that 'it is an error to suppose that mud is pleasant when it does not stick and that lies do not matter as they are not true'. In frivolous mood he substituted his own wife's name in Shaw's exhortation, 'in short dear Nancy, let yourself rip and wear all your pearls'. His mock indignation was given full vent when Shaw wrote of his shock on discovering a new stop on the organ of St Mark's, Venice. 'It is a trumpet. Not the horrible English trumpet, (which is like a cheap accordion trying to imitate a braying donkey and only succeeding in being a bastard cornet)'. 'I USED TO PLAY AN ACCORDION'. JJ protested in capital letters at the back of the book.

Asked about the big 'ifs' of his life, what he might have done if he had not become a millionaire business man, he invariably replied that he would have liked to have arranged his life in three chapters. As a young man he ardently wished to be a champion swimmer. In middle age he would have liked to have been a landscape gardener and in old age a philosopher, searching for wisdom.

In his twilight years aspiration coincided more nearly with reality. He had time now to 'think, to wonder, to dream' as he put it. He had long been captivated by the story of ancient Greece. There was a civilisation which richly fed his imagination in the Greeks' exciting quest for truth in mathematics, the art of politics and love of philosophy. 'God is always doing geometry', said Plato. From

Socrates he may have taken his persistent questioning, awesome to some, especially late at night. The word 'philanthropy' itself is derived from the Greek. Aristotle, who was very critical of oligarchies and of the rich as a class, praised the generous man, who prized his wealth not for its own sake but as a source of his giving to others. Philanthropists in the city states provided corn, oil and money for the needy, gave prizes and books in many fields of instruction and bursaries or assisted placed to scholars. They subsidised important social activities like the public baths and gymnasium. JJ's constant reference to a 'community chest' for Bristol could well have been derived from his reading of Greek history.

Too realistic to be an uncritical hero worshipper, he was attracted to one great hero from the golden days of fifth-century Athens – Pericles. The leader's idealistic speeches, coloured by Thucydides, had a great resonance for John James. In his funeral oration for the dead in the first year of the Peloponnesian war Pericles praises the liberality of Athens; the law is impartial, public distinction is given to merit, not to party or class: in social matters toleration reigns and in public matters there is self-restraint and an absence of violence. Athens too is rich in spiritual, intellectual and material things of civilisation.... In Athens wealth gives opportunity for action, not for boasting, and it is idleness, not poverty, which is disgraceful. A man has time for both his private affairs and for the affairs of the city, and those engaged in business are yet quite competent to judge political matters. 'The man who can best be accounted brave is he who best knows the meaning of what is sweet in life and what is terrible, and then goes out undeterred to meet what is to come'.

With characteristic provocation JJ loved to argue that Pericles was a greater man than Winston Churchill. JJ had never seen life through rose coloured spectacles but an old man could be allowed to dream that perhaps one day Bristol, warts and all, might emulate the culture and the civic qualities of Athens in the Golden Age.

In the months after his return home he still maintained his tenacity of spirit, though ageing. He realised that he had to keep his diary all the more meticulously. His conversation, perhaps not as focused as at the height of his powers, was still scattered with questions, sometimes on the meaning of life and death. He had always admired the extraordinary self discipline of Mahatma Gandhi. He had a respect for the transcendental. He enjoyed his talks with his grandson, David, who had become a Buddhist, asking him about his journey to Khatmandu and about the teachings of Krishnamurti, a spiritual teacher who had established a flourishing centre in Hampshire.

Shortly before Christmas 1995 David came from his home in South Wales to play his grandfather at chess as he had done for many years on his visits to Tower Court. He noticed his grandfather's increasing weakness but JJ summoned all his mental powers, pored over his chessboard made of marble with the elegantly carved pieces, concentrated extremely hard and kept his unbeaten record against his grandson.

Family and friends visiting at this time all discerned his stoic calm in facing the end, which came quietly at home in the presence of his closest family on January 31st, 1996. Some thirty years earlier he had observed that serenity was the prize of old age. It was the greatest prize that he was profoundly grateful to have. John James died a contented man, at peace with himself and the world.

*　*　*　*

His funeral took place very quietly at Canford, Westbury on Trym, attended by his immediate family, intimate friends and colleagues, whose journeys were hampered by a fall of snow. His daughters Pat and Joan were there. Pat's daughter, Sally, had travelled from the USA. His son David had died there some months earlier. The arrangements were made by the former Archdeacon of Bristol, Leslie Williams, a friend of the family and a participant in their weddings and baptisms. The press were carefully excluded but when the news broke the obituaries soon appeared in the national and local press. The letters of sympathy flowed in to the family and to the *Western Daily Press* and *Evening Post*, which printed a little of the moving correspondence from people whose lives he had touched under the banner heading, 'we must always remember John'. 'A truly modest man and a great Bristolian'. One correspondent who had worked as a 17-year-old girl in the office over his shop in 1947 concluded, 'I could go on for hours but another thing I learned from JJ was not to use three words where one will suffice'.

The Service of Thanksgiving for his life and work was held on Friday 3rd May, appropriately at the beautiful Church of St Mary Redcliffe, less than half a mile from his birthplace in Philip Street. The historic church on its 'red cliff' had welcomed home Bristol's famous adventurers as they sailed up the Avon and had seen the start of countless voyages of exploration and trade. Had he lived a little longer he would have been thrilled by the celebratory 'Festival of the Sea' with nearly a thousand ships moored nearby, and the voyage to Newfoundland of the brand new version of Cabot's 'Matthew'.

Now the civic procession led by the Lord Mayor walked past a Guard of Honour at the porch, provided by members of the Normandy Veterans' Association and the Old Comrades Branch of the Coldstream Guards. A crowded congregation included representatives of every age and facet of the community, Cabinet Minister and Bristol West Member of Parliament, William Waldegrave, heads of schools, hospital and medical service chiefs, Merchant Venturers, old age pensioners, nurses and children's charities.

The organ played one of his favourite popular songs, Frank Sinatra's 'My Way' before the service began in more traditional manner with hymns, including 'There is a green hill far away' from his childhood days, and prayers. Mrs Joan Bourns read a poem that had been sent to the family by one of his nurses. The lesson from Ecclesiasticus began, 'Let us now praise famous men, and our fathers in their generations' going on, as JJ would have approved, to humbler people 'who have no memorial, who have perished as though they have not lived.... But these were men of mercy, whose righteous deeds have not been forgotten'.

Charles Clarke, prominent leading citizen and Merchant Venturer, described the boy from Bedminster and painted a portrait of the man of great ability and tenacity, who gave away his money, initially to the elderly for their outings. 'If you are living and barely managing on a small pension with no frills, imagine the looking forward, the happy, cheerful day, the looking back in warm retrospect. What a splendid thing to do'. His talents and gifts entitled him to 'take a proud place amongst the historic benefactors of this city, the saintly William Canynges, builder (among others) of this lovely church, Edward Colston, now of the controversial reputation, Sir George White, whose immense contributions to the life of the city deserves a revival of interest, and many of those forward thinking ideas he shared with John, the Wills family to whom the University is due!

His family may take great pride in his achievements. We think today of his devoted daughter, Joan, her sister Pat and the grandchildren and great grandchildren; of John's sister, Ann and her family; we ask them to be consoled by our sympathy, our pride and our gratitude.

It is an old truism that only when one of our friends is dead do we learn the details of his achievements and realise what he meant to us. We are here today to pay tribute to a Great Man and to be grateful that we have been able, by his vision and the use of his talents to see a little closer to the heart of things'.

His name would certainly live on through the work of his Trusts. The Dawn James Trustees now had to continue to grapple with the complex problems of a fast changing society with mounting demands for the welfare of the vulnerable, the sick, the elderly and under privileged. It was time to tackle a major problem and make an important decision on their priorities. Was the Old Folks' Festival now out of date?

In August 1996 the Trustees announced with very great reluctance their decision to end the Festival. 'Times have changed and we need to rethink the use of the Funds which are set aside for the Festival and to reallocate them. The Trustees were now able to announce 'We have donated £1,000,000 to the Appeal Fund for the new Children's Hospital, which is being planned in the St. Michael's area. This sum will be used to buy the latest modern equipment to give local children and others the very best treatment. We have also donated £250,000 to BRACE to help Professor Gordon Wilcock with the good work he is doing relating to Alzheimers and other diseases which affect many elderly people'. These were magnificent donations to support a National Health Service desperately needing funds in crucial areas.

The End of a Life 1994–6: The End of the Century

The Dawn James Trust was now based in a substantial Victorian house in Redland to which it had moved on leaving Minster House in 1989. A fine portrait of JJ by James Scrase hangs in the hall as if the subject were busy at his desk but able to look up and appraise critically every visitor with those sharp eyes. Family photographs, plaques and shields which commemorate gifts and celebrations from grateful recipients, decorate the walls of meeting rooms and offices. On the landing hang framed verses by his sister, Anne, who wrote a poem every year for her brother's birthday.

Miss Elizabeth Pennington retired from her outstanding service to him in business and trust activities, as did Mrs Gloria Powney. In 2000 AD the chairmanship of the Trust is held by Mrs Joan Johnson who succeeded her father. Appeals for help arrive daily from every quarter and are read carefully and sympathetically before being presented to the Trustees.

On 30th September 1998 the Dawn James (No.2) Charitable Foundation was officially closed, the whole of its capital being transferred as expendable endowment to the John James Bristol Foundation, the transfer amounting to £9,911,236. The latter Foundation in his name had been set up in 1983 on very similar lines to the original Dawn James Trust for 'the relief of poverty and sickness, and to aid the advancement of education in Bristol'.

The Trust could face the challenge of the 21st century in good heart. In 1999 the *Evening Post* launched a competition to discover Bristol's 'Person of the Century'. Readers were first asked to nominate the men and women of their choice, among them the politicians, the sportsmen and women, the entertainers, the charity workers, the medical pioneers, inventors and benefactors. It was a list of which any community would have been proud. John James came top in people's estimation, winning a landslide victory with 59 per cent of the votes, the nearest candidates registering less than 10 per cent.

The discussion on the respective merits and achievements of the candidates and the results elicited a magnanimous letter from Sir George White, great grandson of the versatile founder of Bristol Aircraft Company, pioneer of local transport, philanthropist and donor of the Edward VII wing of the Bristol Royal Infirmary of which he was chairman. The great grandson pointed out many similarities in the stories of two great men, John James and Sir George, their rise from poverty as docker's and painter and decorator's sons, their love of their native city. Of his own great grandfather he observed regretfully but truthfully 'yet only 83 years after his death very few Bristolians really know who he was or what he did'.

He concluded his full and striking appraisal with a call to action. 'John James has shown himself through the *Evening Post* to be a hero of our time. He is a role model of real distinction and fresh in Bristolians' memories. Let us hope that Bristol as a city will find an ingenious and worthy way in which it can keep that memory alive'.

For John James himself 'the respect and affection of my fellow Bristolians' were the greatest reward he could envisage. He had surely earned it.

Appendix A

'My Grandfather'

These original notes entitled 'My Grandfather' were written in 1966 by Jacqueline Fiddick to record important events in the life of John James Senior, father of John and of her mother, Ann. He was much loved by his family.

> John James was born in 1884, his parents were not well off, nobody was in those days, his father worked on the Docks stacking timber. He had five brothers and one sister. He was born in Stone's Buildings, Stillhouse Lane, and when he was three he went to the Zion Chapel School where they taught him to sew, later he went to the Bright Bow School next door to the Police Station in Bedminster, which consisted of two rooms, and then to the Corporation School when it was built in Stillhouse Lane. He loved playing down by the docks, and saw his friend drown there when he was five. His brother was also drowned the year of Queen Victoria's Golden Jubilee. The Dock men used to chase the boys away, but they still came back again.
>
> Also when he was five he went into hospital for a time, and when he came out the church sent him and another group of boys to a small village by the sea side, just outside Truro for about four weeks, to convalesce. They used to go on the beach each day, and go to the services in the church, the Vicar's daughter looked after them. He used to play cricket on the village green, and remembers the long train journey there and back again. When he was seven his family moved to the first house

on the left in the Tennis Court, halfway up Redcliffe Hill. In the evenings he used to run all the way to the Clock Shop (half way up Redcliffe Hill) to see the time on the clock over the doorway, and then run home again to tell his father so that he could set the alarm clock. One day when he was doing this, a young man asked him if he knew where Mr James lived, and it turned out to be his brother Ted, who he had never seen before. Ted had been out in India in the army but had now left and come home. They put him up sleeping rough on the floor and later he got a job on the Docks, but after a time he left and went to Wales and got married.

When John was ten he left school and ran away to Wales to find his brother and his wife. He stayed with them for a while but they sent him home again because he broke a chicken's leg by kicking a football. He never went back to school again, but got a job selling newspapers for halfpenny each; he made one and a half pence for each dozen he sold, and used to stand near a bus stop and take a long time finding the right change in the hope a bus would come along and the customer would say 'keep the change'. He also worked for a greengrocer who used to deliver goods around Windmill Hill, holding the horse's head for him; he was so small at that age, that when the horse shook his head it used to send him flying, he got a shilling a week for doing that. Later he went to work for J. C. Wall as a van boy, he got four and sixpence a week; when he was twelve years old he was promoted to two horses and they gave him five shillings a week. Later still he was promoted to the transfer berth where he earned seven and sixpence per week with twopence an hour overtime plus one and sixpence if he packed more than the others, and he did this so often that they always put him down for the extra one and sixpence.

He started courting at ten; his girlfriend used to live in a court in Princes Street which was near King Street

Appendix A 133

where they were then living (after leaving the Tennis Court the family moved to Merricks buildings at the bottom of Redcliffe Hill near the alms houses, later still they moved to Clark Street and then to King Street, it was cheaper than paying rent). He used to give all his money to his mother, but kept his overtime money, and he and his girlfriend, Clara[1] Hayward, (sometimes wearing old stockings) used to go to the old Theatre up in the gallery for twopence and have a penny bun and a bottle of pop, and drop crumbs on the people below; they saw plays like Maria Martin in 'Murder in the Red Barn' and 'The Bells'. There were no queues for tickets in those days, as soon as the doors were opened you all had to rush, and sometimes you got pushed down and trampled on. (He later married this same girlfriend he courted at ten.)

When he was fourteen he ran away again to Wales to work in the pits, with a friend of his. They crossed over on the Marchioness of Cardiff, the fare was then ninepence, and caught a train up to where he remembered an Aunt of his lived. He only had four and sixpence on him. His Aunt took him in, but told his friend to go home again as he looked dirty and she thought he might have fleas. He got a job working down the Pit carrying the loosened coal over to the big metal drum in a tub with two handles, the big drum later took the coal to the surface pulled by a pit horse. He kept to this job until his father died and he went back to Bristol for a time. He was then sixteen. He got a job in the South Liberty Pit in Bristol but the pay was so poor that he left that and for a time worked with horses for Jenkins, but finally he went back to Wales again as the money was better over there. He had a very fine singing voice, and used to entertain the miners a lot by singing in the different Clubs. He didn't drink much, and he used to give his free beer ticket (payment for his singing) to his

[1] Also known as Emily

friend, a big Irishman, who would drink his beer for him.

He was well liked by the miners, and always good for a laugh, but one of his jokes misfired completely and almost got him the sack. He had rigged up an electric wire, which he threaded down the sleeve of his jacket and into his hand so no-one could see it, so that when somebody touched it they would get a shock. He then started to spin his friends one of his stories and at the end of it, when they were all laughing, the man in charge of the pit-horse picked up the pin to attach the horse to the drum. He put his hand on the drum whilst he did this and that was when John touched the wire to the side of the metal drum. The man got a shock and jumped a mile and everyone began to laugh, but the poor old pit-horse also got a shock and it bolted off down the pit. There was rising water at the bottom and the poor horse fell in and drowned; there was an awful row about this and directly work was over he was told to go and see the head of the firm, D Davies & Son. He thought that he'd have the sack on the spot, but luckily the Boss had heard of him and how he used to entertain the people at the Buffs by singing to them, and after a severe warning, he gave him another chance.

He had many strange experiences whilst working in the mines. Once he had volunteered to stay down in the pits whilst they drained off the water. The water that dripped into the mines was allowed to run under the planks the miners walked on and into a big pit under the cage, and every so often they would empty this pit out, by lowering the cage onto it and filling up a big tank inside the cage, and hauling up the cage and emptying it. Whilst he was down there all alone he suddenly saw two green lights coming towards him out of the shaft; they were quite low to the ground and moved quite slowly and he was terrified. Then suddenly it miaowed and he saw that it was a cat, and he was never more relieved in his life. Once too there was a blockage at the mouth of the pit and he and his friends had to walk for miles underground, all through the disused mines running under the mountains; they came up in another mine many miles from their own village.

When he was twenty one he was working down the pit when suddenly the cage that carried the men up and down the mines, fell on him. Nobody thought he could survive the terrific weight of the cage falling on him, but luckily his head fell into a groove in the floor, which saved his neck from being broken, but nearly every other bone in his body was broken and he was squashed flat by the weight of the cage. They carried him to his lodgings and operated on him straight away on the kitchen table, and strapped up his ribs with sticky tape like stripes, so that he looked like a sergeant. For a long time he couldn't move and his body and face were black with bruises, but finally his family and girl friend came to fetch him and he went back to Bristol where he rested a further twenty two weeks before he was able to start looking for a job again. The first job he got was on the Docks carrying sugar, but later he went to work for the Western Counties again where later he was made Foreman. He got married about 1905 when he was twenty one, and both he and his wife walked to the Wedding and got there late and all the guests had gone home. He had a hard job to persuade the Vicar to marry them, but finally he did, and they walked home again; none of their friends would believe them though, when they told them that they actually had got married because they'd left too early. He and his wife went to live in two rooms at Mrs Cox's but later moved to 96 Philip Street. They had two children, a boy and a girl, and they had been married thirteen years when in 1918 his wife died in the Big Flu Epidemic; his youngest child aged six, went to live with her Grandmother in the same street and he looked after his son. At this time he was still working on the Docks as a docker. He worked there all through the war loading and unloading the ships.

Both his children were very bright and both passed the Scholarship to the Grammar School, but he could only afford to pay for his son's education and he sent him to the Merchant Venturers' Grammar School on this scholarship. He was still in the 'Buffaloes' at this time and every year they went to Weston for the day. At 18 his daughter came home and looked after the house and cooked his meals. He was a strict father though and she had to be in by 10 p.m. each night. His son at this time joined the Air Force falsifying his age to get in, as a Wireless operator, whilst he started work at the Holm Sand and Gravel Company. His son would send him money home each week, but he never spent it, just put it in the bank for him when he left the RAF. Both his son and his daughter got married, but his daughter stayed with him for a time when the last War started. During the War he went into hospital for a hernia operation and they found he had another hernia in his stomach, probably caused by the pit accident years before. They also found he had pernicious anaemia, but all they could tell him to do then was to eat raw liver, and he went to Fleet to stay with his daughter to recover.

His daughter had two children and his son had four, and after the War his son left the RAF and bought his own radio shop and started his own business and gradually expanded until he owned many shops and became a Multi-Millionaire. He bought his Father a house near to where his Father's daughter (his sister) lived, but John James Snr, still owned the house in Phillip Street that he had bought many years before, and he let it to the people who used to live in the top room. Then one day, when he was down at his old house repairing it, he tripped and fell down the stairs breaking his ankle. He didn't want to worry the people there, so he walked on it right up the road until he got to the police station. They called an ambulance and took him to Hospital, and actually this broken ankle saved his life, as whilst he was there they too discovered that he had Pernicious

Anaemia, and they asked him if he would be the Guinea Pig for a new drug they had just discovered which they hoped might cure it, called B.12. First of all they sprayed it into his mouth. Then they gave him tablets but these did not work, so they gave him an injection, but this time it was too strong and his blood began to clot; for a time he was seriously ill, as a blood clot passed right across his brain, but he survived again, and later they worked out the exact amount needed for him. From that time to this day he still has an injection once a month, which keeps him alive.

He lived all alone in the house for many years after he retired, and then in 1962 his daughter moved into a new house with a large garden. They had a small house built in the garden specially for him so that he could grow his tomatoes. His grandchildren grew up and most of them got married; to date he has six great grand children, and a greenhouse full of tomatoes. He is now over 82.

Jacqueline Fiddick
1966

Appendix B

Ann regularly wrote a poem like this to send to her brother on his anniversary

> To JJ on his 82nd birthday.
> Another year has come and gone
> so here's a little birthday song.
> Your Empire sold, no backward glance
> at stocks and shares, you take a chance
> To send the old folk on their trips
> give clever kids their scholarships.
> To give the surgeons tools, not pills
> to cure their patients of their ills.
> So keep on with your plans and schemes
> whilst other men sit dreaming dreams.
>
>   From his sister Ann. 1988.

Appendix C

An extract from John James' personal photograph album from Malta days with his own narrative.

NOVEMBER, 29TH. 1924.
ENGLAND — CAPE TOWN FLIGHT.
SIR ALAN COBHAM IN HIS SINGAPORE ALL METAL FLYING BOAT REACHED CALAFRANA BAY. MALTA DURING A SPELL OF STORMY WEATHER. THE BOAT WAS SUITABLY MOORED BUT THE WEATHER INCREASED IN VOILENCE

2.
It was impossible to get the boat ashore owing to the lack of cradles or runners for such a huge craft. The heavy swell was still rising making the position a very dangerous one. As a last resort it was decided to beach the boat.

3.
The task was going to be no small one — rain was falling and one wing was badly smashed up leaving the machine a pitable object.

Appendix C

4.
WORK-A-DAY CLOTHES WERE EXCHANGED FOR SWIMMING
COSTUMES AND IN AN EFFORT TO BALANCE THE MACHINE
SEVERAL FELLOWS PERCHED THEMSELVES ON ONE OF THE LOWER WINGS
THUS THE STRUGGLE COMMENCED.

5.
A STOUT ROPE WAS TAKEN FROM THE FRONT COCKPIT TO
THE SHORE AND A TUG OF WAR AGAINST THE WIND
RAIN AND TIDE ENSUED

6.
SLOWLY, AND WITH AS MUCH CARE AS POSSIBLE IT WAS DRAGGED SHOREWARDS—FOR WITHIN THE NEXT FEW MONTHS THIS FLYING BOAT MUST FLY THOUSANDS OF MILES

7.
RAIN STILL FELL AND EVERYONE WAS WET TO THE SKIN — BUT THE PRIZE AT STAKE WAS TOO GREAT TO ALLOW OF ANY SLACKING. ROPES WERE FASTENED TO THE WING AND ONE LAST EFFORT WAS NEEDED.

Appendix C

Another hour's struggle and, the largest flying boats in the world was safe from any immediate danger. Battered and torn it was intact save for the left wing.

Appendix D

My first thanks for their great help go to Mrs Ann Fiddick and Mrs Joan Johnson, John James' sister and daughter.

Thanks for his reminiscences of the early days to Mr Arthur Webb who was a member of staff, 1946–1981.

My gratitude also to the following for their kind assistance: Sir Alun Talfon Davies, Maurice Furnell, Sir Julian Hodge, David Johnson, Maureen Jones, David Miller and John Parkhouse.

Messrs Beasant, Marks & Cole, Mr & Mrs Fido and others of the Bedminster Memories Group, Mr D. W. Allen and Mr W. K. Campe residents at Farnborough, the Librarian and Information Officer at RAE, the Keeper of Research and Information at RAF Museum, Hendon, Professor Roy Niblett and Mr Eric Packer, Mr John Williams, City Archivist and his staff, the Librarian and Staff at College Green, Bristol.

Mrs Joan Bourns, St Peter's Hospice, Mr Derek Bond, The Guild of Guardians, Mr R. Brown, The Greater Bristol Foundation, Brigadier H. W. K. Pye, The Merchant Venturers' Society and Mr Michael Smith, Filton High School, Headmaster (ret).

My gratitude also to people, too numerous to mention.

For photographs including:

Associated Newspapers, *Bristol Evening Post*, Mrs M. L. Cooper, Maureen Dunn, Financial Times Ltd., James Russell & Sons, Ken Bray Studios, Reece Winstone, South West Picture Agency Ltd., Strutt & Parker, The Society of Merchant Venturers, University of Bristol Faculty of Arts and M. Wallis & Associates.

For quotations including:

Bristol Evening Post, Charles Clarke, David Beasant, David Higham Associates Ltd., Financial Times, *London Evening News* (Associated Newspapers), the *Guardian*, The Institute of Economic Affairs, The Malago Society/Malago Publications, The Society of Merchant Venturers, the *Sun* (News Group Newspapers Ltd.), and the Western Daily Press.

Bibliography

Many articles and reports in the local and national press and journals, too numerous to mention individually. The family scrap book contains over 160 pages including articles in:

> The *Bristol Evening Post*, The *Bristol Evening World*, The *Western Daily Press*, The *Financial Times*, *The Times*, *The Sun*, *The Sunday Times*, *The Observer*, *The Guardian*, The *Daily Mail*, The *Daily Mirror*, *Electrical and Radio Trading Journal*, *Electrical and Radio Training*, *Business*, The *Stock Exchange Gazette*, The *Investors' Chronicle*, The *Statist*, *Electrical Weekly* and *Wireless and Electrical Trader*.

Other sources include:

> Judgement: Birkett v. James Queens Bench Division 19 March, 1979.
>
> Bristol Old Folks' Festival Committee Minutes, 1963–79.
>
> Clarke, Charles, Address at Memorial Service May 3rd 1996.

And books including:

> Avery, J. R. *While We Have Time*. pub. Queen Elizabeth Hospital. 1990
>
> Booker, Christopher, *The Seventies* Allen Lane 1980
>
> Bullock, Alan, *The Life and Times of Ernest Bevin*
>
> Bungay, Joan, *Redland High School 1882–1982* R.H.S Council, 1983

Burgess, R, Collard, R, Ogden, D, *Where the Fat Black Canons Dined*, Bristol Cathedral School, 1992

Davies, Norman, *Europe* OUP 1996

Dunn, Sarah, *The First Hundred Years – Colston's Girls' School* Redcliffe Press, 1991

Elliot and Atkinson, *The Age of Insecurity* Verso 1998

Hands, A. R. *Charities and Social Aid in Greece and Rome*

Hill, C. P. *The History of Bristol Grammar School 1532–1986* Alan Sutton, 1988

Johnson, Paul, ed. *20th Century Britain, Economic, Social and Cultural Change*

Kitto, H. D. F. *The Greeks* Penguin 1951

Leasor, James. *Wheels To Fortune – The Life and Times of Lord Nuffield*, The Bodley Head, 1954

Leech, Roger, ed. *The Topography of Medieval and Early Modern Bristol*, Bristol Record Society Vol. XLVlll, 1997

McGrath, P. V. *The Merchant Venturers of Bristol* 1975

Miller, Harry, *The Way of Enterprise* analysis of 21 post war British Firms. Published for the The Institute of Economic Affairs by André Deutsch

Morgan, Kenneth, *Colston and Bristol* Bristol Branch of the Historical Association, 1999

Morgan, Kenneth, *The People's Peace 1945–89* OUP 1998

Nielson, W. A. *The Golden Donors* pub. Tonman Tally/New York 1985

O'Sullivan, Timothy, *Julian Hodge* Routledge and Kegan Paul 1981

Pelling, Henry, *Modern Britain 1885–1955* Nelson 1960

Pratten, D. G. *Tradition and Change* The Story of Cotham School

Bibliography

Pudney, John, *Laboratory of the Air*

Smith, J. H. *Water under the Bridge* Memories of a Bedminster Man

Taylor, A. J. P. *The Oxford History of England 1914–45*

Turnill and Reed, Farnborough. *The Story of RAE*

Vear, L. G. W. *Bedminster Boy, Bedminster Between The Wars, South of the Avon*

Vanes, Jean, *Apparelled in Red*, Red Maids School 1984

Watson, S. J. *Furnished with Ability – The Life and Times of the Wills Family*. Dulverton Trust 1991